# BOEING 707
## PIONEER JETLINER

HK-749

RENÉ J. FRANCILLON

MBI Publishing Company

First published in 1999 by MBI Publishing Company, 729 Prospect Avenue, PO Box 1, Osceola, WI 54020-0001 USA

MBI Publishing Company books are also available at discounts in bulk quantity for industrial or sales-promotional use. For details write to Special Sales Manager at Motorbooks International Wholesalers & Distributors, 729 Prospect Avenue, PO Box 1, Osceola, WI 54020 USA.

Library of Congress Cataloging-in-Publication Data

Francillon, René J.
  Boeing 707 : pioneer jetliner / René J. Francillon.
      p.  cm. – (Jetliner history)
  Includes index.
  ISBN 0-7603-0675-3 (pbk. : alk. paper)
  1. Boeing–History. I. Title II. Series.  TL686.B65F73  1999
  629.133'349–dc21
               99-28954

**On the front cover:** After being stored following test completion in January 1970, the 367-80 was donated to the National Air and Space Museum, Smithsonian Institution, in May 1972. Due to lack of space, the 367-80 could not be displayed in the nation's capital, and it was stored at Davis-Monthan AFB, Arizona, for 18 years. Once again refurbished, it was flown over Boeing plants during the company's 75th anniversary celebration in 1991 before being placed in temporary storage at Plant 2, Boeing Field, in Seattle. *Boeing*

**On the frontispiece:** Already carrying its Pan American N708PA registration, the first production 707 is shown in its test livery. First flown on 20 December 1957, this aircraft was delivered to Pan American World Airways on 30 November 1958. Re-engined with JT3D-1 turbofans in February 1965 as a 707-121B, this aircraft crashed on Chances Mountain, Antigua, West Indies, on 17 September 1965. *Boeing*

**On the title page:** Delivered to Lufthansa as D-ABON in January 1962, this 720-030B was acquired by Pan American in December 1965. Almost seven years later it was bought by AVIANCA. It was photographed in the markings of this Colombian carrier at Quito, Ecuador, in September 1975. It was withdrawn from use and stored at Bogota, Colombia, in May 1982. *René J. Francillon*

**Back cover, top:** In addition to serving as the development aircraft for the 707 and 720 series of jetliners and military derivatives, the Boeing 367-80 also led to the production of 820 C/KC/RC-135s for the USAF and the French Air Force. Built as a C-135B-04-BN and delivered to the USAF in June 1962, serial 62-4135 was modified to RC-135M standard in 1966-67 and became a RC-135W in November 1980. In the later style, it is shown landing at Nellis AFB, Nevada, on 18 September 1991. *René J. Francillon*

**Back cover, bottom:** S/N 19870 was delivered to Continental Air Lines in April 1968. Sold to VARIG in March 1972, this 707-324C is shown taxiing at the Jorge Chávez IAP in Lima, Peru, in May 1977. Acquired by the Força Aérea Brasileira in March 1987, it was subsequently modified by Boeing as a tanker with Beech refueling pods beneath the wingtips. *René J. Francillon*

Edited by Mike Haenggi
Designed by Tom Heffron

Printed in Hong Kong

# CONTENTS

# ACKNOWLEDGMENTS

When I undertook to write this history of the *Boeing 707: Pioneer Jetliner,* I did not realize that I was embarking on a cruise "down memory lane." My first job in the air transportation industry was as a traffic agent trainee at Orly Airport in Paris in November 1956, at a time when the Boeing 367-80 demonstrator had notched only 502 flights and logged only 611 hours and 25 minutes. Its manufacturer, The Boeing Company, was then considered primarily a military aircraft manufacturer with unbeatable experience in bomber aircraft design but with little savvy in the airliner business. Until October 1956, when it overtook the Douglas Aircraft Company in jetliner sales (with book orders for 135 Boeing 707s versus 115 Douglas DC-8s at the end of that month), its forays in the commercial field had been marginally successful.

In 1961, while researching the doctoral dissertation I had started before emigrating to the United States, I wrote to the four leading aircraft manufacturers to request documentation on their airliners. Written in broken English, my requests received mixed answers: Convair sent a few pages of limited professional value; Douglas and Lockheed contributed a few glossy brochures; but Boeing came through as a champion by sending a heavy cardboard box loaded with detailed information. Among these documents was the personal copy of a technical report which a kind and understanding public relations representative entrusted to a young and unknown foreign student. I am indebted to my generous Boeing friend for the kind loan of this document. Performance charts reproduced from this report helped me twice. First, in 1964, they impressed my faculty mentors when I defended my dissertation successfully to earn a Ph.D. in Air Transportation Economics. Thirty-four years later, they again proved most useful when working on this book.

Also gathering dust in my garage were Boeing documents accumulated over the years while I was working for the competition (engineers fleeing the damp Pacific Northwest in search of California sunshine brought along marvelous "goodies" most appreciated by Douglas colleagues; the reverse flow was equally useful to our Boeing friends) and later planning and designing civil airports where aging 707s often were the critical design aircraft. Among the most useful Boeing documents resurrected from my garage was a 1967 listing titled *Announced Turbine Transport Sales* from which all sale dates and numbers appearing in this book were extracted.

To supplement the 707 files covering some 10 linear feet of garage shelving, I was most fortunate to receive unstinting support from Mike Lombardi and Tom Lubbesmeyer, the knowledgeable and most helpful Boeing Historical Archivists. They deserve much of the credit for this book.

A hoist of long-time friends from around the world contributed information, illustrations, and technical assistance. I am most grateful to one and all. Special thanks go to Mark Meredith for his superb drawings, Michael MacKay for patiently helping again and again to tame my computer, and to Dr. Richard K. Smith. Dick is a genuine aviation historian, not a buff. As such, over the past 30 years, his analytical skills and his teaching of the importance of weights within the "zero-sum" system of what he calls the Weight Envelope as a critical element in the success, or lack thereof, of airliners have broadened my understanding of commercial aviation.

Finally, I am grateful to my long-suffering editor, Mike Haenggi for awaiting manuscript, illustrations, and galley corrections while I twice abandoned my writing task to return to air transportation consultancy.

I hope that you will enjoy reading this book as much as I enjoyed writing it. 'Twas fun remembering being young when jetliners came onto the scene.

# INTRODUCTION

Between July 1927, when the two-passenger (plus pilot and mail) Model 40A was placed in service by Boeing Air Transport Inc. as the first Boeing airliner, and April 20, 1952, when the Boeing board of directors approved the expenditure of $16,000,000 for the development of the 367-80 transport/tanker demonstrator, the Seattle firm had built only 249 passenger transports. Eighty of these aircraft were single-engined Model 40s and 281s, 15 were three-engined Model 80/226s, 76 were twin-engined Model 247s, 12 were four-engined Model 314 flying-boats, and 66 were pressurized four-engined Model 307s and 377s.

Pan American ordered the first 707s in October 1955; Just five short years later, Boeing posted more airliner orders than in that 25-year period between 1927 and 1952. (The epoch-making order was for three 707-320s placed in November 1960 by

Air France, the third 707 order from the French carrier.) The Boeing Company was on its way to becoming the world's leading manufacturer of airliners.

Moving on from success to success, the Seattle-headquartered firm went on to develop the 727 trijet (first flown on February 9, 1963), the 737 twinjet (flown on April 9, 1967), the 747 jumbo (flown on February 9, 1969), the narrow-bodied 757 twinjet (first flown on January 13, 1982), the wide-bodied 767 twinjet (first flown on September 26, 1981), and the very large capacity 777 twinjet (flown on June 12, 1994) with only limited competition until the European Airbus consortium effectively challenged the Boeing dominance in the late 1990s. Notwithstanding that competition, Boeing remains the world leader.

By the end of January 1999, the company had sold 14,245 jetliners, 12,496 of which had been delivered. (These totals, however, included 3,503 DC-8s, DC-9s, DC-10s, MD-11s, MD-80s, MD-90s, and Model 717s sold by Douglas/McDonnell Douglas prior to and after their takeover by Boeing.) Of the 10,627 genuine Boeing jetliners and derivatives sold by that date, 9,068 had been delivered to commercial, government, and military customers. Few companies can brag about a greater success story!

Assessments of the impact of the Boeing 707 on world air transportation may differ from one side of the Atlantic to the other, reflecting parochial attitudes. Whereas in the United States the National Air and Space Museum of the Smithsonian Institution designated the Boeing 367-80 prototype of the Boeing jetliner one of the 12 most significant airplane designs of all time, in Britain three noted writers appraised the 707 less glowingly. In their *Jet Airliner A to Z* survey serialized in the monthly *AIR International*, Bill Gunston, Jon Lake, and Gordon Swanborough notably wrote "Though an excellent design, the aircraft actually owed its pre-eminence as much to luck as to its inherent excellence." That pre-eminence was, in fact, due to a combination of heavy jet experience and years of jetliner studies.

By the spring of 1952, when Boeing took the decision to proceed with the manufacture of its 367-80 demonstrator, the company had a 220,000-pound (100-ton) jet bomber (the B-47) in production and in service with the United States Air Force, and a 390,000-pound (176.9-ton) strategic jet bomber (the B-52) that had just been flown and concurrently was moving into production. No other manufacturer in the world came close to having as much experience in the design and serial production of jet aircraft in excess of 100 tons.

Furthermore, Boeing had spent 5 1/2 years working and re-working a bewildering number of designs for jet transports and jet tankers, continuously revising them relative to available engine thrust. Concurrently, as analyzed in chapter 2, in 1952 and thereafter, Boeing was operating under the "educational" competitive pressures applied by Douglas (wider fuselage for more productive operations and greater range for intercontinental operations), and Convair (higher cruise speeds and turbofan engines). Contrary to this complex scene, a flippant estimate of "luck" can hardly explain the *phenomenal success* of the Boeing 707 jetliner.

The same British authors also noted in their survey that the 707-120 ". . . had been incapable of long-range transoceanic operations with full payload and the early services to Europe had been little more than public relations exercises." True, the 707-120 lacked the range for nonstop transatlantic operations but the only other jetliners then in service—the de Havilland Comet 4 and Tupolev Tu-104—both were even less capable. Although the Comet 4 was credited with a greater still air range than the 707-120 (4,080 miles/6,565 kilometers versus 3,380 miles/5,440 kilometers), the Comet 4 was slower (typical cruising speed being 480 miles per hour/772 kilometers per hour versus 535 miles per hour/861 kilometers per hour), carried fewer passengers (67 versus 111 in typical 1958 two-class configurations), and had a narrower cabin (123 inches/3.12 meters for five-abreast seating economy accommodation versus 148 inches/3.76 meters with six-abreast seating). Moreover, as noted in chapter 3, initial 707-121 operations by Pan American World Airways resulted in near capacity loads in spite of fares much higher than those charged by airlines in the late 1990s. In the world of business, of which air transportation is part, such profitable operations can hardly be described as "little more than public relations exercises."

The Tu-104 was a dismal economic failure and owned its very existence and long service life to political necessities. Finally, neither the British Comet 4 nor the Soviet Tu-104 had the growth potential of the American 707. Battling stiff competition from Douglas and its DC-8 (which had even a greater growth potential), Boeing totally outperformed its rivals. Ending up building 1,010 of its 707s, 720s, and military derivatives between 1954 and 1991, the Seattle manufacturer nearly outsold all other manufacturers of first generation long-range and intercontinental range jetliners.

The *combined* output of Convair, de Havilland/Hawker Siddeley, Douglas, Tupolev, and Vickers/BAC was 1,077 aircraft. This includes 556 DC-8s, 202 Tu-104s and Tu-110s, 163 Comets and Nimrods, 102 Model 880s and Model 990s, and 54 VC10s. And the total from these five manufacturers and three national sources is only 67 aircraft more than the 1,010 Model 707/720s produced by a single factory in Renton, Washington. Some "bloody luck" indeed!

# CHAPTER ONE

# DEVELOPMENT OF A WINNER

The oldest preliminary layout drawing for a jetliner to have survived in Boeing's archives is dated December 9, 1946. Drawn by W. L. Kellerman, this layout featured a high-mounted swept wing, swept tail surfaces, four turbojets in underslung twin pods, and a tricycle undercarriage. Overall length and span respectively were 107 feet 6 inches (32.77 meters) and 116 feet (35.36 meters). Indeed, the concept and layout of this undesignated aircraft were well ahead of their time, while the size of this conceptual aircraft, not remarkable by today's standard, was above the contemporary norm.

Prototype of the third type of jetliner to enter airline service, the Boeing 367-80 is one of the most important designs in the history of world civil aviation. It is shown here as it appeared in early 1962 after being re-engined with JT3D-1 turbofans and fitted with leading-edge flaps during boundary layer control testing. *Boeing*

(The four-engined Douglas DC-4 which entered service in 1946, just when Boeing was beginning to sketch a jetliner concept, had an overall length of 93 feet 5 inches/28.47 meters.)

Before studying the evolutionary development which led from this unnamed preliminary project to the introduction into service of the 707-121 12 years later, it is appropriate to review briefly the status of jet engine development and major trends in airline operations during the late forties and early fifties as they explain the problems faced by Boeing and its competitors when developing the first generation of jetliners.

## The First Jet Aircraft

Development of turbine engines was pioneered in the late thirties and got a boost with the start of hostilities. In Great Britain, Frank Whittle first bench-tested its W.U. (Whittle Unit, an experimental turbojet expected to have a static thrust of 1,200 pounds or 5.34 kiloNewtons) on April 12, 1937. In Germany, bench test-running of the 550 pounds thrust (2.44 kN) Heinkel HeS 1 turbojet was initiated in September 1937. Test flying of the

Previous Spread: Sharing the ramp at Boeing Field with B-52Cs, the 367-80 is being readied for another test flight. The almost fully opened aft cargo door is noteworthy. *Boeing*

HeS 3A began in early 1939 with a 992-pound thrust (4.41 kN) turbojet slung beneath the fuselage of Heinkel He 118 V2, the second prototype of an unsuccessful two-seat dive bomber powered by a Daimler-Benz DB 600 liquid-cooled engine. In the United States, where the military had expressed interest in reaction propulsion as far back as 1922, no concrete developments had taken place. World War II accelerated British and German developments and, at last, prompted the United States into action.

The first turbojet-powered aircraft to fly was the Heinkel He 178 V1. Powered by a Heinkel HeS 3B and piloted by Flugkapitän Erich Warsitz, this experimental aircraft made a brief hop over the runway at Marienehe on August 24, 1939. Its first full flight took place on August 27, 1939, just five days before World War II started with the German invasion of Poland. The next jet-engined aircraft to fly were the Italian Caproni-Campini C.C.2 with a propellerless Isotta-Fraschini radial engine driving a ducted-fan compressor inside its fuselage; the German He 280, the world's first twinjet; the British Gloster E.28/39; and the German Me 262 V3, the prototype of the world's first operational jet. At that time, America's first jet aircraft was yet to fly.

To catch up, America first undertook to have General Electric build a version of the Whittle W.2B engine, for which they

# World War Two Jet Aircraft Chronology

| Aircraft | First Flight Date/Location | Pilot | Remarks |
|---|---|---|---|
| Heinkel He 178 V1 *(Germany)* | August 27, 1939 Marienehe | Erich Warsitz | Skip hop on August 24, first full flight on August 27. |
| Caproni-Campini C.C.2 *(Italy)* | August 28, 1940 Taliedo | Mario de Bernardi | |
| Heinkel He 280 V1 *(Germany)* | April 2, 1941 | Fritz Shäfer | |
| Gloster E.28/39 *(U.K.)* | April 8, 1941 Hucclecote | P.E.G. Sawyer | Skip hops on April 8, first full flight on April 15 at RAF Cranwell. |
| Messerschmitt Me 262 V3 *(Germany)* | July 18, 1942 Leipheim | Fritz Wendel | Prototype of the world's first operational jet fighter. |
| Bell XP-59A *(USA)* | October 1, 1942 Muroc Dry Lake | Robert Stanley | |
| Gloster F.9/40H *(U.K.)* | March 5, 1943 RAF Cranwell | Michael Daunt | Prototype of the Meteor jet fighter. |
| Arado Ar 234 V1 *(Germany)* | June 15, 1943 Rheine | Flugkapitän Sell | Prototype of the world's first jet reconnaissance/bomber aircraft. |
| de Havilland E.6/41 *(U.K.)* | September 20, 1943 Hatfield | Geoffrey de Havilland | Prototype of the de Havilland Vampire jet fighter. |
| Lockheed XP-80 *(USA)* | January 8, 1944 Muroc Dry Lake | Milo Burcham | Prototype of the Shooting Star fighter. |
| Arado Ar 234 V8 *(Germany)* | February 1, 1944 Rheine | | Prototype of the world's first four-engined jet aircraft. |
| Lockheed XP-80A *(USA)* | June 10, 1944 Muroc Dry Lake | Tony LeVier | First flight of an aircraft powered by a U.S.-designed turbojet. |
| Junkers Ju 287 V1 *(Germany)* | August 16, 1944 Brandis | Siegfried Holzbauer | Prototype of the world's first medium jet bomber. |
| Heinkel He 162 V1 *(Germany)* | December 6, 1944 Vienna-Schwechat | Flugkapitän Peter | Prototype of mass-produced "people's fighter." |
| McDonnell XFD-1 *(USA)* | January 2, 1945 Lambert Field, St. Louis | Woodward Burke | Prototype of the Phantom, the world's first carrier jet fighter. Single-engined skip hop on January 2 and full flight on January 26. |
| Bell XP-83 *(USA)* | February 25, 1945 Buffalo | Jack Woolams | |
| Nakajima Kikka *(Japan)* | August 7, 1945 Kisarazu | Susumu Takaoka | |

were offered a contract on September 4, 1941, two months before Japan forced the United States into the war. The next day, Bell agreed to design an aircraft around this jet engine. The resulting twinjet XP-59A was first flown by Robert Stanley at Muroc Dry Lake in the Mojave Desert of California on October 1, 1942. Even though they were powered by improved engines, the limited-production Bell P-59As and P-59Bs were nowhere close to operational standard. However, at last they had gotten America into the running.

Over the next two years, the pace of jet aircraft development picked up, and by the time World War II ended, no fewer than 15 types of jet aircraft had been flown, 6 in Germany, 3 in Great Britain, 4 in the United States, and 1 each in Italy and Japan. However, only the German Me 262 (beginning in April 1944 with *Erprobungskommando* 262), the German Ar 234 (with the fifth and seventh prototypes assigned in July 1944 to 1. *Staffel, Versuchsverband Ob.d.L*), and the British Meteor (first with No. 616 Squadron in July 1944) had been flown operationally. Four Lockheed P-80As were shipped to Europe at the end of 1944 but were not used operationally, and the first USAAF jet aircraft unit scheduled for deployment to the Pacific was still in training when Japan surrendered.

The largest and heaviest jet prototype to fly during the war had been the Junkers Ju 287 V1. Powered by four 1,984 pounds thrust (8.82 kN) Junkers Jumo 004B-1 axial-flow turbojets and featuring forward swept wings, this aircraft had a span of 65 feet 11.75 inches (20.11 meters), a length of 60 feet 0.5 inches (18.30 meters), and a take-off weight of 44,092 pounds (20,000 kilograms). It thus was significantly smaller than the standard twin-engine U.S. transport of the time, the Douglas C-47 (DC-3) and lighter than the standard four-engine transport, the Douglas

Prior to the unconditional surrender of the Third Reich, Germany was the undisputed leader in jet development. In July 1944, its Messerschmitt Me 262A-1a became the world's first operational jet fighter. The Me 262B-1a/U1 was a two-seat night fighter variant with FuG 218 Neptun V radar with *Hirschgeweith* antenna array. *AAF*

Experience gained by Boeing with the six-jet B-47 and eight-jet B-52 proved invaluable for the company during the more than seven-year gestation of its first jetliner. Built as a RB-47H, but shown after being modified as a radar and navigation system testbed for the General Dynamics F-111, this aircraft (53-4296) became the last Stratojet in USAF service. *USAF/AFFTC*

Placed into service over the North Atlantic in November 1955, 16 months after the first flight of the 367-80, the Lockheed 1049G Super Constellation enabled TWA to offer for the first time nonstop service "across the pond" when winds were favorable. Boeing had failed to realize the importance of non-stop transatlantic service and initially offered its 707 with insufficient range performance. *Lockheed*

C-54 (DC-4). Postwar, the size and weight of jet aircraft rapidly increased in the United States as test and development of jet bomber prototypes was initiated in 1946–1947.

The first of these aircraft was the twinjet Douglas XB-43 which flew on May 17, 1946, but was not placed into production. Next came the prototypes of four competing designs developed to meet USAAF requirements for jet-powered medium bombers. Flown respectively on March 17, 1947 and April 2, 1947, the North American XB-45 and Consolidated-Vultee XB-46 were both powered by four turbojets but, in other respects, were conventional. Also retaining straight wings, the Martin XB-48 was airborne on June 22, 1947, becoming the world's first aircraft to fly on the power of six turbojets. (The second prototype of the Junkers Ju 287 had been designed to be powered by six turbojets but was uncompleted when Germany surrendered in May 1945. Completed in the Soviet Union, the Ju 287 V2 also flew in 1947, possibly before the XB-48.) Also powered by six turbojets and first flown on December 17, 1947, the Boeing XB-47 was far more innovative, as it had swept

Also developed as a result of Brabazon Committee recommendations, the de Havilland Comet represented a giant leap forward in terms of airliner development. Registered G-ALZK, this aircraft was the second development aircraft ordered by the Ministry of Supply in 1946. When it first flew in July 1950, one year after the first Comet, Boeing was still nearly two years away from deciding to build its 367-80 demonstrator. *de Havilland*

wings. Boeing went on to build 1,629 B-47s (to which were added 274 Stratojets built by Douglas and 386 built by Lockheed), thus gaining the experience needed to develop successful jetliners. Completing this series of early U.S. jet bombers was the eight-jet Northrop YB-49 flying wing, which first flew on October 21, 1947.

## U.S. Jet Engine Development

After investigating the practicality of jet propulsion for the Air Service Engineering Division, Edward Buckingham of the National Bureau of Standards had concluded in 1922 that there was "no prospect whatsoever that jet propulsion . . . will ever be of practical value, even for military purposes." Thereafter, with the exception of a few visionaries, American officers, engineers, scientists, and industrialists failed to devote significant attention to turbine-engine research.

Notable exceptions came from two aircraft manufacturers in Southern California, Lockheed Aircraft Corporation and Northrop Aircraft, Inc., which both commenced work on turbine engines in 1939. The foresight of these two firms remained unrewarded as their very advanced designs—that from Lockheed being the twin-spool, axial-flow L-1000 turbojet expected to generate as much as 5,000 pounds thrust (22.2 kN) while that from Northrop was for the Turbodyne axial-flow propeller turbine engine which eventually developed 10,000 shaft horsepower (7,460 kiloWatt)—did not progress past the development stage. Since the Lockheed L-1000

was never completed and only three Northrop Turbodyne prototypes were bench tested in 1947, America ended up having to rely on British assistance and the capabilities of its industrial turbine manufacturers to get into the jet age.

In answer to a three-month-old request from Major General Henry H. "Hap" Arnold, Chief of the U.S. Army Air Corps, the National Advisory Committee for Aeronautics (NACA, the forebear of today's National Aeronautics and Space Administration or NASA) had set up a Special Committee on Jet Propulsion in March 1941. Less than a month later, early taxi tests of the Gloster E.28/39, Britain's pioneering jet aircraft, were witnessed by Gen. Arnold. While the NACA Special Committee on Jet Propulsion asked Allis Chalmers, General Electric (GE), and Westinghouse, the nation's leading industrial turbine manufacturers, to participate in the committee's investigation, Gen. Arnold secured British assistance. Thereafter, things began to move faster.

On September 4, 1941 General Electric was asked, and agreed, to build 15 "Type I superchargers" based on the Whittle W.2B turbojet design. (The letter "Eye" designation of the "Type I supercharger" was chosen to give the appearance that GE, which was then manufacturing turbosuperchargers for contemporary aircraft engines—such as the Type B fitted to the Wright R-1820 radials powering Boeing B-17s—would merely be working on an improved turbosupercharger.) Type I bench-testing started in Lynn, Massachusetts, on April 18, 1942, and a pair of Type I-A engines powered the Bell XP-59B on its first flight on

Undoubtedly most graceful, the de Havilland Comet 4 (shown here in the markings of East African Airways) and its Comet 4B and 4C derivatives never had a chance to shine once the Boeing 707 entered service. *de Havilland*

Starting late in the race to develop jetliners, the Soviets pulled "a rabbit out of the hat" by developing the Tu-104 transport from their Tu-16 jet bomber and placing it into service 25 months before the Boeing 707. That aircraft, given the NATO reporting name "Camel," did not prove economical in service with Aeroflot and CSA.

October 1, 1942. General Electric went on to develop uprated versions of the Type I—the I-14, I-16, and I-20—but it was a de Havilland Halford H.1B turbojet imported from Great Britain which powered the Lockheed XP-80, the first American single-jet aircraft, on its January 8, 1944 maiden flight.

Two months before General Electric had begun adapting the Whittle design to U.S. specifications as the Type I, the three industrial turbine manufacturers which had been supporting research by the NACA Special Committee on Jet Propulsion had been awarded development contracts. Navy contracts went to Allis Chalmers for the development of a ducted-fan engine and to Westinghouse for turbojets. An Army Air Forces contract went to General Electric for the design of a turboprop engine. The Allis Chalmers ducted-fan engine did not pan out, and the General Electric TG100, which in May 1943 became the world's first turbine propeller engine to be bench tested, ended up powering only the Consolidated-Vultee XP-81 (the first turboprop-powered flight in the United States was made on December 21, 1945, just two months after the experimental Gloster Meteor-Trent had become the world's first turboprop aircraft to fly in England). More successful, the series of small diameter turbojets developed by Westinghouse resulted in the WE-19XB-2B powering the first USN carrier jet, the McDonnell XFD-1 Phantom, on its maiden hop on January 2, 1945. A development of the WE-19, the first American axial-flow turbojet, went on large-scale production as the J34 for naval fighters.

While working on improved models of the Whittle turbojet and on its TG100 turboprop, General Electric took an early lead in U.S. turbojet development by incepting two turbojet designs with an initial rating of around 4,000 pounds thrust (17.8 kN). First bench tested in January 1944, the I-40 centrifugal-flow turbojet powered the Lockheed XP-80A, the production prototype of the Shooting Star, on its first flight in June 1944. Redesignated J33 and mostly built under license by Allison, the I-40 became the first American turbojet engine to be mass produced. Even more successful, the General Electric TG-180 axial-flow turbojet was built in large numbers as the J35, mostly by licensees Allison and Chevrolet.

Having paid scant attention to the potential of turbine engines prior to the war, the three traditional aircraft engine manufacturers in America—Allison, Pratt & Whitney, and Wright—had been instructed by the War and Navy Departments to concentrate their

Photographed in September 1975 at the Mariscal Sucre Airport in Quito, Ecuador, this Caravelle VI-N in the markings of the private Ecuadorian airline SAETA had been originally delivered as a Caravelle III to Alitalia in June 1960. The Caravelle short-range twinjet was a contemporary of the Boeing 707. *René J. Francillon*

activities on their established piston engine lines once it became likely that America would be drawn into the war. This they did with conspicuous success, with Pratt & Whitney and its licensees manufacturing some 356,000 engines between July 1940 and August 1945, while Wright and licensees built 223,000 radial engines and Allison added 69,000 V-1710 liquid-cooled engines. However, when the war ended, Allison, Pratt & Whitney, and Wright were left to catch up with turbine technology. At first, Allison fared a bit better, as it had been selected as a licensee for General Electric J33 centrifugal-flow and J35 axial-flow turbojets, but Pratt & Whitney and Wright had to turn to Britain to get into the turbojet engine business.

Pratt & Whitney started negotiating for manufacturing and sales rights for the Rolls-Royce Nene in April 1947, eight months after the original American licensee, the Taylor Turbine Corporation, had acquired initial rights in this centrifugal-flow turbojet. Wright, which initially favored turboprop engines, was even slower to grasp the turbojet potential and only acquired

license rights for the Armstrong Siddeley Sapphire axial-flow turbojet after war had broken out in Korea.

Thus, when Boeing initiated preliminary design of jetliners in late 1946, the leading turbojets available in the United States were the Allison-built J33 and J35 and the Pratt & Whitney JT6, the civil variant of the J42 American military derivative of the Rolls-Royce Nene. None of these engines appeared to be sufficiently fuel-efficient to power commercial transport aircraft, but proposed JT6 and JT7 versions of the Nene, with static thrust of up to 7,000 pounds (31.1 kN), appeared the most promising.

## The Post-World War II Airline Boom

In 1946, when Boeing began preliminary design work on jetliners, the air transportation industry was much different from what it is today. At the beginning of the year, all-important transcontinental routes linking East Coast cities (mainly New York, but also Boston, Philadelphia, and Washington) with Los Angeles and San Francisco were still operated with unpressurized, twin-engine Douglas DC-3s in 16 to 20 hours, depending on the number of intermediate stops. During 1946, the introduction of four-engine aircraft (unpressurized Douglas DC-4s and pressurized Lockheed Constellations) enabled fiercely competing trunk carriers to operate transcontinentally with only one intermediate stop and to fly the 2,500-mile (4,000-kilometer) routes in 13 to 14 hours with DC-4s and 11 hours with Constellations. Eastbound transcontinental service was not offered until October 1953, when TWA began 1049C Super Constellation service between Los Angeles and New York in less than 8 hours. Westbound, nonstop scheduled service began in November 1953 when American Airlines introduced the Douglas DC-7, making the flight against prevailing winds in 8 1/4 hours.

Other routes that played a significant part in determining the payload-range characteristics of the first generation of jetliners were those across the North Atlantic. Although limited passenger service had been initiated with a Boeing 314 flying-boat first taking 22 passengers from New York (Port Washington) to Marseilles, France, in June 1939, sustained service only commenced after the war. Five airlines (American Export, BOAC, Pan American, TCA, and TWA) offered multi-stop service with landplanes (Douglas DC-4s for the U.S. airlines and Avro Lancastrians for the British and Canadian carriers). Critical legs were between either Shannon, Ireland, or Prestwick, Scotland, and Gander, Newfoundland (the Shannon-Gander leg was 1,715 nautical miles/3,177 kilometers, uncorrected for prevailing winds from the west). Over the North Atlantic, new and more capable aircraft were introduced in January 1946 (Lockheed Constellation by Pan American), June 1949 (Boeing Stratocruiser by Pan American), May 1952 (Douglas DC-6B by Pan American), October 1953 (Lockheed 1049C Super Constellation by TWA), November 1955 (1049G Super Constellation by TWA), June 1956 (Douglas DC-7C by Pan American), June 1957 (Lockheed 1649 Starliner by TWA), and September 1957 (turboprop-powered Bristol Britannia 312 by BOAC).

North Atlantic operations still required at least one stop until November 1954, when Pan American began flying nonstop eastbound with Stratocruisers fitted with additional fuel tanks. Westbound nonstop flights between London or Paris and New York became possible only with the introduction by TWA of the 1049G Super Constellation in November 1955. Even then, winter winds and/or heavy payload often still required a refueling stop. By then the 367-80 had already accumulated 336 flight hours, and Pan American had placed its historical order for the first 20 Boeing 707s.

After World War II ended, all U.S. and international services were offered in a single class. However, coach fares were introduced on selected routes in the United States at the end of

With U.S. trunk airlines, the Vickers Viscount outsold the later and more capable Lockheed Electra. The largest U.S. customer for the Viscount was Capital Airlines, which ordered 75 of these turboprop-powered airliners. Capital's Viscounts were later repainted in the markings of United Airlines (as shown by this photograph of an ex-Capital Viscount 745 taken at the Washington-National Airport in November 1967). *René J. Francillon*

Built as a demonstrator for both a military tanker/transport and a civil jetliner, the Boeing 367-80 was provided with main-deck cargo doors forward and aft of the left wing. In this photograph, taken shortly after the aircraft had been rolled out at the Renton plant, the aft cargo door can be seen barely ajar. *Boeing*

the introduction of tourist fares was appreciated, and six years before economy class was first offered on North Atlantic routes. This helps to explain why Boeing initially planned its jetliner with fuselage cross-section optimized for four-abreast first and five-abreast tourist accommodation and without nonstop transatlantic capability.

## British Challenge

Credit for introducing turbine-powered aircraft into airline service goes to Great Britain. Both the jet-powered Comet and the turboprop-powered Viscount resulted from the inspired work of the Brabazon Committee. Chaired by Lord Brabazon of Tara, this committee had been set up by the British Government in December 1942 to make recommendations for the postwar development of airliners, a task made even more challenging by the fact that British transport aircraft manufacturers had fallen behind even before wartime needs forced them to concentrate on the design, development, and production of combat aircraft.

1948 and were extended to transcontinental services one year later. On North Atlantic routes, tourist fares and economy fares were introduced in May 1952 and April 1958 respectively. The impact of these lower fares was dramatic. The number of passengers carried by the nine airlines then offering scheduled service between North America and Europe (Air France, BOAC, KLM, Pan American, Sabena, SAS, Swissair, TCA, and TWA) jumped from 329,656 in 1951 to 432,272 in 1952. Nevertheless, in 1952, only 4 out of 10 North Atlantic passengers traveled by air. Five years later, with the availability of cheaper fares (73.4 percent of the air passengers traveled in tourist class in 1956), air transportation finally overtook sea transportation across the North Atlantic. In 1958, the introduction of economy class and jet service resulted in yet another jump in air traffic over the North Atlantic, with the number of air passengers first exceeding the 1 million mark in that year.

Work on the 707 was thus begun when transatlantic service was still offered with one or more stops, before the full impact of

Reporting between August 1943 and November 1945, the second Brabazon Committee came up with recommendations for five classes of airliners.

Type I called for the development of a 300,000 pound (136,080 kilogram) aircraft for nonstop operations between London and New York. Ill-inspired, this specification resulted in the behemoth Bristol Brabazon landplane and Saro Princess flying-boat, neither of which proceeded past the prototype stage.

Type II was tailored to European operations. It resulted in the design of three aircraft: the Airspeed Ambassador which, powered by a pair of radial engines, was built in limited number and failed to match the success of the Convair 240/340/440 series; the experimental Armstrong Whitworth Apollo powered by four turboprop engines; and the Vickers Viscount.

Type III aimed at an aircraft optimized for operations on the Empire routes (i.e., those linking Britain with colonies in Africa,

Taken on the ramp at Boeing Field after the 367-80 had been retrofitted with the fin-tip probe antenna of the 707, this photograph shows the progress achieved between the 1931-vintage, 10-seat, single-engine Pilgrim Model 100-A and the pioneering Boeing Jetliner. *Boeing*

Asia, and the Pacific). It resulted in the Avro Tudor which, powered by four liquid-cooled engines, was intended as an interim aircraft pending availability of the jet-powered Avro 693. Although development of the perhaps overly ambitious Avro 693 was canceled in 1947, it is worth noting that its design ultimately called for a wing area of 2,700 square feet (250.8 square meters), more than 10 percent larger than that of the 707-120 which entered service in 1958.

Type IV began as a specification for a relatively small jet-powered aircraft to transport mail over the North Atlantic. However, it ended up as the brilliant de Havilland Comet, the world's first jetliner, which was initially built for operations over the Empire routes.

Type V resulted in two types of feeder liners, the de Havilland Dove and the Miles Marathon.

Several of the recommendations by the Brabazon Committee fell wide of the mark. However, as its members had recognized that British turbine engine manufacturers then had a substantial lead over their American competitors, they also resulted in the turboprop-powered Vickers Viscount and turbojet-powered de Havilland Comet. With these two aircraft, Britain heralded a new era in air transportation.

## The First Jetliners

Originally projected as a jet-powered North Atlantic mailplane—a singularly ill-conceived plan to obtain a successor to the four-engined, float-equipped upper component of the prewar Short Mayo—the Brabazon Type IV evolved into the commercially more justified D.H.106. In the process, de Havilland moved away from the originally considered twin-boom configuration inspired by its D.H.100 Vampire jet fighter and from an even more innovative tailless, swept-wing design (for which the ill-fated D.H.108 was to have provided data). Adopting a remarkably clean layout with a pressurized fuselage and moderately

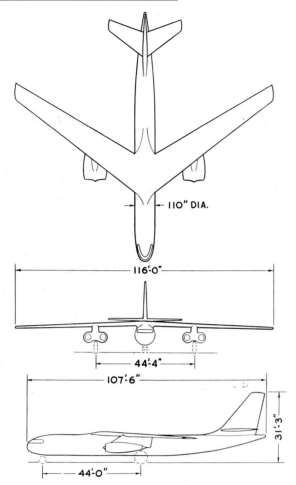

110" DIA.

116'-0"

44'-4"

107'-6"

31'-3"

44'-0"

Dated December 1946, this three-view drawing of the first Boeing jetliner layout shows the B-47 influence with jet pods and shoulder-mounted wings. *Boeing*

swept wings with four de Havilland Ghost turbojet engines buried in their roots, de Havilland ended up designing an aircraft no longer meeting Brabazon Type IV requirements for a North Atlantic mailplane. Instead, the revised D.H.106 to Specification 22/46 met Type IIIA requirements for a medium- to long-range turbine-powered airliner for use on the Empire routes.

Two D.H.106 prototypes were ordered by the Ministry of Supply in May 1946. Eight months later British Overseas Airways Corporation (BOAC) placed a preliminary order for eight aircraft on January 21, 1947, thus becoming the world's first airline to step into the jet age. The first prototype flew at Hatfield on July 27, 1949 and was first shown publicly at the Society of British Aerospace Companies (SBAC) Show less than two months later. Although generating much

interest, the novel Comet initially failed to attract additional orders, as airlines felt that the new jetliner with first-class accommodation for up to 36 passengers would be too expensive to operate, making it difficult to turn in a profit or even to break-even. However, a series of record flights between London and European capitals at average speeds above 420 miles per hour (675 kilometers per hour) soon demonstrated that the Comet was likely to have high passenger appeal. Before the first 36-seat production aircraft was delivered to BOAC on April 2, 1951, export orders for eight Comet 1As were received from Canadian Pacific Airlines and two French carriers (UAT—Union Aéromaritime de Transport—and Air France).

After setting records between London and European capitals, the Comet 1 was ready for commercial operations. Carrying 36 passengers, the first production Comet left London on May 2, 1952 bound for South Africa. After five intermediate stops, it landed the next day in Johannesburg after covering 6,724 miles (10,819 kilometers) in 23 hours 34 minutes.

First flown on February 16, 1952, the Avon-powered Comet 2 proved more attractive to prospective customers, and orders for this longer-ranged version were placed by Air France, BOAC, British Commonwealth Pacific Airlines, Canadian Pacific, Japan Airlines, Línea Aeropostal Venezolana, Panair do Brasil, and UAT. Unfortunately, before Comet 2s could be delivered to airlines and before the Comet 3 prototype flew on July 19, 1954, six of the pioneering Comet 1s had crashed or been destroyed, with the loss of 99 passengers and crew members.

As evidenced by the following table, Britain had not been the only country to realize that the development of turbine-engined transports offered a unique opportunity to challenge the U.S. hegemony.

While most of the early aircraft in this table were jet-powered testbeds, the Avro Canada C.102 Jetliner was a genuine transport aircraft intended for one-stop service between Montreal and Vancouver. Conceived in Great Britain, but designed, built, and flown in Canada, the C.102 Jetliner was the recipient of a letter of intent issued in April 1946 from Trans-Canada Airlines (TCA). However, non-availability of the planned Rolls-Royce Avon turbojets forced the manufacturer to substitute four less powerful and more fuel-thirsty Rolls-Royce Derwent turbojets. Performance fell significantly below those for the projected twin-Avon version, and TCA lost interest before the first flight of the Derwent-powered Jetliner on August 10, 1949.

More importantly, design of the SNCASE (later Sud and then Aérospatiale) Caravelle had been initiated in France before Boeing and Douglas committed to building jetliners. Stemming from a request for proposals issued in November 1951 by the French government, the twinjet Caravelle was intended for

## Jet Transport Testbeds and Jetliners Chronological Listing by First Flight Date: The First 15 Years

| Type | First Flight Date | First Revenue Operations | Number Built | Number Remaining in Airline Operations in 1998 |
|---|---|---|---|---|
| Avro Lancastrian-Nene (U.K.) | Aug 8, 1946 | Testbed | 1 | None |
| Vickers Nene-Viking (U.K.) | Apr 6, 1948 | Testbed | 1 | None |
| Avro Tudor 8 (U.K.) | Sep 6, 1948 | Testbed | 1 | None |
| De Havilland Comet (U.K.) | Jul 27, 1949 | May 2, 1952 | 114 | None |
| Avro Canada C.102 Jetliner (Canada) | Aug 10, 1949 | Prototype | 1 | None |
| Vickers Tay-Viscount (U.K.) | March 15, 1950 | Testbed | 1 | None |
| Avro Ashton (U.K.) | Sep 1, 1950 | Testbed | 6 | None |
| SNCASO SO 30R-Nene & SO 30P-Atar (France) | Mar 15, 1951 | Testbed | 2 | None |
| Chase XC-123A (USA) | Apr 21, 1951 | Testbed | 1 | None |
| **Boeing 367-80** (USA) | **Jul 15, 1954** | **Prototype** | **1** | **None** |
| Sud Caravelle (France) | May 27, 1955 | May 12, 1959 | 282 | None |
| Tupolev Tu-104/Tu-110 (USSR) | Jun 17, 1955 | Sep 15, 1956 | 202 | None |
| **Boeing 707** (USA) | **Dec 20, 1957** | **Oct 26, 1958** | **763** | **120** |
| Douglas DC-8 (USA) | May 30, 1958 | Sep 18, 1959 | 556 | 253 |
| VEB Baade Type 152-I (East Germany) | Dec 4, 1958 | Prototypes | 2 | None |
| Convair 880 (USA) | Jan 27, 1959 | May 15, 1960 | 65 | None |
| **Boeing 720** (USA) | **Nov 23, 1959** | **Jul 5, 1960** | **154** | **1** |
| Convair 990 (USA) | Jan 24, 1961 | Mar 9, 1962 | 37 | None |
| De Havilland Trident (U.K.) | Jan 9, 1962 | Mar 11, 1964 | 117 | None |
| Vickers VC10 (U.K.) | Jun 29, 1962 | Apr 29, 1964 | 54 | None |

**NOTE:** The Lancastrian-Nene was a jet engine testbed obtained by replacing the outboard Rolls-Royce Merlin liquid-cooled engines of Lancastrian serial VH472 with Rolls-Royce Nene turbojets. After being fitted with the two jet engines, VH472 first flew on 8 August 1946. A few days later, it was flown on turbojet power alone. Again flying on the Nenes alone, VH472 became the "world's first jet airliner" on September 19, 1946 when media representatives and Air Ministry officials were taken aloft. On November 18, 1946, once again taking-off, flying, and landing without using the Merlins, VH472 flew from London to Paris-Le Bourget in a record time of 50 minutes. During that flight, top speed was 263 miles per hour (423 kilometers per hour), a remarkable achievement considering that the Lancastrian I only reached a maximum of 230 miles per hour (370 kilometers per hour) when flying on the power of all four Merlin piston engines. The return trip from Villacoublay was made in 49 minutes.

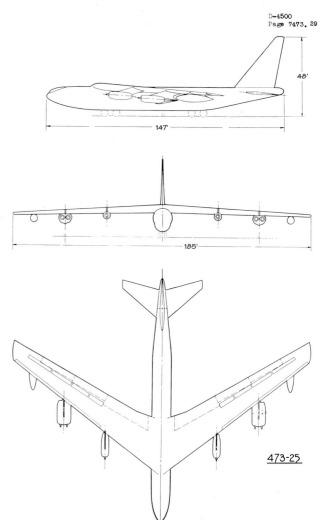

D-4500
Page 7473. 29

48'

147'

185'

473-25

Within a few months, Boeing Model 473 evolved from the conservative 473-11 twin-jet design to the ambitious 473-25. The latter clearly showed its Model 464-67 (XB-52) parentage. *Boeing*

operations on European, Middle Eastern, and North African routes. Selected as one of the three finalists in March 1952, one month before the Boeing board authorized development of the 367-80 tanker/transport demonstrator, the Caravelle first flew on May 27, 1955, 10 months after the 367-80.

## American Reactions

While at first the French challenger was not taken seriously in the United States, the turbine-powered British designs elicited serious interests from several U.S. trunk carriers and from Pan American. Capital Airlines, a trunk carrier which was acquired by United Airlines in 1961, ordered the first three of an eventual fleet of 75 Vickers Viscount turboliners in May 1954. It initiated Viscount service in the United States in July 1955, 3 1/2 years before the Lockheed Electra became the next turboliner in U.S. service. Orders from Continental Airlines and Northeast Airlines eventually resulted in 147 of the 445 Viscounts built by Vickers being delivered to U.S. airlines. This was indeed a rather remarkable achievement for the British aircraft industry, particularly in the light of the fact that Lockheed only built 170 turboprop-powered Electras and never quite matched the Viscount in the home market (144 Electras were delivered to U.S. carriers).

When BOAC inaugurated scheduled jet service on May 2, 1952, U.S. airlines lost their apathy toward jetliners. Four months later, R. E. Bishop, director and chief engineer for de Havilland, arrogantly proclaimed during the SBAC Show, "We feel we have a lead on the Americans of between four and five years on jet transport aircraft. They are now in the same position we were in 1946." This boasting, however, failed to take into account the tremendous industrial power of the American aircraft manufacturers. R. E. Bishop had to eat crow as his company's inability to boost production rates cost prevented it from securing lucrative U.S. orders.

Among those in attendance at the 1952 SBAC Show were G. T. Baker and E. V. Rickenbacker, presidents respectively of National Airlines and Eastern Air. As the payload/range performance of even the original Comet 1 were sufficient for operations on the New York–Miami routes on which their airlines competed fiercely, Messrs. Baker and Rickenbacker were ready to order Comets. In particular, Eddie Rickenbacker planned an initial order for 35 to 50 Comets, provided that de Havilland would deliver these aircraft within two years from contract. That did not prove feasible and, even before a series of disasters struck the Comet 1 and led to its permanent grounding in April 1954, de Havilland had lost all chances for more than a token penetration of the U.S. market.

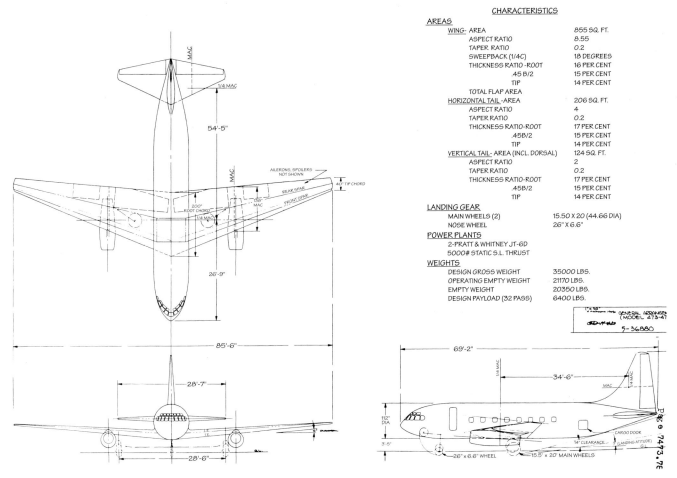

## CHARACTERISTICS

AREAS
| WING- | AREA | 855 SQ. FT. |
|---|---|---|
| | ASPECT RATIO | 8.55 |
| | TAPER RATIO | 0.2 |
| | SWEEPBACK (1/4C) | 18 DEGREES |
| | THICKNESS RATIO -ROOT | 16 PER CENT |
| | .45 B/2 | 15 PER CENT |
| | TIP | 14 PER CENT |
| | TOTAL FLAP AREA | |
| HORIZONTAL TAIL -AREA | | 206 SQ. FT. |
| | ASPECT RATIO | 4 |
| | TAPER RATIO | 0.2 |
| | THICKNESS RATIO-ROOT | 17 PER CENT |
| | .45B/2 | 15 PER CENT |
| | TIP | 14 PER CENT |
| VERTICAL TAIL- | AREA (INCL. DORSAL) | 124 SQ. FT. |
| | ASPECT RATIO | 2 |
| | TAPER RATIO | 0.2 |
| | THICKNESS RATIO-ROOT | 17 PER CENT |
| | .45B/2 | 15 PER CENT |
| | TIP | 14 PER CENT |

LANDING GEAR
| MAIN WHEELS (2) | 15.50 X 20 (44.66 DIA) |
|---|---|
| NOSE WHEEL | 26" X 6.6" |

POWER PLANTS
2-PRATT & WHITNEY JT-6D
5000# STATIC S.L. THRUST

WEIGHTS
| DESIGN GROSS WEIGHT | 35000 LBS. |
|---|---|
| OPERATING EMPTY WEIGHT | 21170 LBS. |
| EMPTY WEIGHT | 20350 LBS. |
| DESIGN PAYLOAD (32 PASS) | 6400 LBS. |

GENERAL ARRANGED
(MODEL 473-47
5-36880

With the 473-47 layout, Boeing temporarily returned to a conservative configuration, one which the company resurrected some 13 years later when designing the mightily successful 737 twinjet. *Boeing*

That penetration came about after de Havilland announced the development of a much heavier Comet version with both greater range and increased payload. Powered by four 10,000 pounds thrust (44.5 kN) Rolls-Royce Avon turbojets instead of the 4,500 pounds thrust (20 kN) de Havilland Ghosts of the Comet 1, this Comet 3 was optimized to carry 50 passengers on single-stop service between London and New York. Consequently, to hedge its bet and be ready to compete with BOAC soon after the British flag carrier was expected to start Comet 3 service, Pan American ordered three of these aircraft on October 20, 1952. However, before the Comet 3 first flew, Comet 1s had to be withdrawn from use due to catastrophic structural failure. By then the 367-80 was about to fly and Pan American prudently canceled its Comet 3 order. Only

one other U.S. carrier, Capital Airlines, showed sufficient interest in the pioneering British jetliner to place an order for four Comet 4s and 10 stretched Comet 4As in July 1956. Two years later, financial difficulties forced Capital to cancel its order for British airliners.

During the late 1940s, while Great Britain forged ahead with its Comet, for which a government order for two prototypes had been awarded in May 1946, U.S. manufacturers of transport aircraft had not remained as idle as R. E. Bishop had made it to appear. True, although undertaking jetliner preliminary studies, the American industry leaders remained lukewarm toward the development of jetliners, as greater benefit would be derived from developing turboprop-powered derivatives of their Super Constellation/Starliner and DC-6/DC-7 series.

Although lacking in performance to be effective tankers for jet bombers, no fewer than 811 piston-engined KC-97s were built for the USAF. After removal of its flying boom and boom operator station, this former tanker served as a C-97E transport with the California Air National Guard during the late sixties. *Peter B. Lewis*

In particular, after studying a 32- to 40-passenger CL-152 with three or four of its own L-1000 turbojets in 1946, Lockheed concentrated its efforts on turboprop-powered aircraft and on flying experimental Super Constellation models powered by Pratt & Whitney T34s (four R7V-2s for the USN, with two becoming YC-121Fs for the USAF and one being re-engined with Allison 501 turboprops). Likewise, for operations over shorter routes, Convair favored turbine developments of its Model 240/340/440 series. First flown on December 29, 1950 after being re-engined with a pair of Allison 501s, its Model 240 prototype became the first U.S. airliner powered by turboprops. However, further turbine development of the 240/340/440 series did not materialize until 10 years later.

Douglas also came close to launching a DC-7D powered by four Rolls-Royce Tyne turboprops but, reacting to customer preference for jet-powered aircraft, the Santa Monica manufacturer announced in August 1952 that it would launch a DC-8 jetliner. Interestingly, this announcement preceded by one month that by Boeing concerning the 367-80. However,

Before starting with a clean sheet of paper to come up with its 367-80/707 design, Boeing studied several re-engined Model 367 developments with turbo-props or turbojets replacing the R-4360 piston engines of the KC-97. The model on the left is a 367-60 with gull wings and T34 turboprops; that on the right, a 367-71 with twin-J57 pods; and that at the bottom, the 367-80. *Boeing*

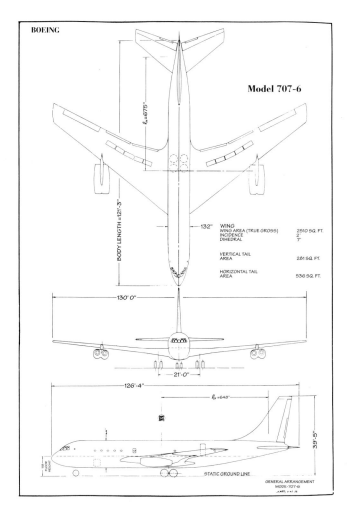

BOEING

**Model 707-6**

ℓ=675"

BODY LENGTH =121'-3"

132" | WING
WING AREA (TRUE GROSS) | 2510 SQ. FT.
INCIDENCE | 2°
DIHEDRAL | 7°

VERTICAL TAIL AREA | 281 SQ. FT.

HORIZONTAL TAIL AREA | 536 SQ. FT.

130' 0"

21'-0"

126'-4"

ℓ=648"

39'-5"

STATIC GROUND LINE

GENERAL ARRANGEMENT MODE-707-6

Dated March 25, 1952, this general arrangement drawing shows the Model 707-6 layout which served as a basis for the 367-80. *Boeing*

perhaps feeling overly confident, Douglas lost the initiative as, unlike Boeing, it sought to wait for airline orders before proceeding with construction of a prototype.

The Air Transport Association (ATA), to which all U.S. scheduled carriers belonged, issued detailed jet transport design recommendations in October 1952. Key recommendations included provision for carrying all fuel outside the fuselage, either in wings or pods or both; undercarriage wells designed to contain damage following tire explosion; ability to operate in 40-miles per hour (65-kilometers per hour) crosswinds; ability to maneuver at low speeds despite failure of one engine in a two- or three-engine aircraft or failure of two engines in a four- or five-engine aircraft; "fail safe" maintenance to preclude incorrect attachment of parts; improved

fire warning and protection; 128-inch (3.25-meter) internal cabin width to make possible five-abreast coach accommodation; and sealed electrical system to eliminate all electrical booby traps.

In the light of later Comet 1 accidents, ATA quite presciently favored individual engine pods and expressed concerns over cabin pressurization problems. In the case of the powerplant, ATA considered it "imperative that the engine installation . . . assure an advancement in the safety of the airplane with respect to fire over that provided in present transport airplanes. An engine fire should not jeopardize the airplane primary structure, adjacent engines, or airplane and engine controls." Concerns over potential structural integrity was expressed by ATA as there was no previous experience in pressurizing so large a volume as the cabin of a jetliner flying at altitude of 40,000 feet.

## ATA Jet Transport Specification

| | |
|---|---|
| Cost per ton-mile | Equal to DC-6 |
| Cruise speed | 550 miles per hour |
| Range, domestic | 2,000 miles |
| Range, international | 3,200 miles |
| Runway length, domestic | 5,500 feet |
| Runway length, international | 7,500 feet |
| Fuselage width, inside diameter | 128 inches |
| Cabin aisle headroom | 80 inches |
| Passenger capacity, first class | 70–80 |

As it turned out, early Boeing 707s and Douglas DC-8s barely met ATA range specifications and failed to meet field-length requirements. On the other hand, they substantially exceeded ATA requirements in terms of cabin width (ATA having issued its specifications six years before economy class was introduced) and seating.

Before detailing Boeing's work leading to the momentous decision to build the Model 367-80 tanker/transport demonstrator, mention must be made of the little known Chase XC-123A. While not a jetliner, this testbed was the first U.S. jet-powered aircraft with a transport-type airframe. Powered by four General Electric J47 turbojets in paired pods under the wing and utilizing the airframe of the second XCG-20 experimental cargo glider, this aircraft first flew on April 21, 1951. However, no further jet development of the C-123 was undertaken, and the type went into production for the USAF with two Pratt & Whitney R-2800 radials as the Fairchild C-123B Provider.

## Boeing Gambles

In the spring of 1947, four months after the undesignated layout mentioned at the beginning of this chapter had been prepared, Boeing initiated more comprehensive preliminary design studies for jetliners under the Model 473 designation. The first of these studies, the 473-1, was a 27-seat, 48,430-pound/21,965-kilogram gross weight aircraft with a tricycle undercarriage and two 6,000 pounds thrust (27.7 kN) Rolls-Royce Nene turbojets in underslung pods. With tanks for only 2,208 gallons (8,358 liters) of fuel, the 473-1 was optimized for domestic operations over sectors of less than 1,200 miles (1,930 kilometers). Within a few days, several other configurations were studied to increase range. Typical of these studies was the 473-11 which, still to be powered by a pair of Nenes, had its wing area increased from 790 to 1,000 square feet (73.4 to 92.9 square meters), carried 2,620 gallons (9,920 liters) of fuel, had a bicycle undercarriage, and range of up to 1,500 miles (2,415 kilometers). As these early 473 configurations had limited payload (with resulting very high seat-mile costs) and limited range (necessitating one or two stops for transcontinental operations), they failed to attract airline interest. However, pending availability of more powerful and more fuel efficient turbojets, there was little that Boeing could do to increase payload and range.

Two years later, experience gained with the six-engined B-47 (first flown in December 1947) and the eight-jet B-52 (for which jet-powered prototypes were ordered in November 1948), together with anticipated availability of civil derivatives of military turbojets in the 7,500- to 10,000-pound thrust (33.4 to 44.5 kN) class, such as the Westinghouse J40 and the Pratt & Whitney J57, enabled Boeing to scale up its proposed jetliners.

Typical of these configurations was the 473-25 detailed in May 1949. Bearing a strong family resemblance with the XB-52 but powered by six instead of eight J57 turbojets, the 285,000-pounds (129,275-kilograms) gross weight 473-25 was planned to carry 98 passengers nonstop across the North Atlantic. Internal and external tanks were to house 18,620 gallons (70,485 liters) of fuel and the 473-25 was expected to have a cruising speed of 530 miles per hour (853 kilometers per hour) at 53,000 feet (16,150 meters). This was a substantial improvement over the performance of early twin-Nene 473 configurations but still a long way from satisfying airline requirements. Notably, the use of shoulder-mounted wings and bicycle undercarriage resulted in the need to retract the four-wheel forward bogie in the fuselage, between the 20-seat forward cabin and the main cabin. Only limited improvements resulted from the adoption of a double-lobe, inverted-eight, fuselage cross section for the 473-29 as housing the two bogies in the lower lobe limited space available for cargo, mail, and baggage.

With the 473-47, Boeing returned in January 1950 to a twin-Nene configuration for domestic operations. Seating was provided for 32 first-class passengers and, with its engines tugged

The rollout of the XB-52 on November 29, 1951 and the first flight of the YB-52 on March 15, 1952 boosted Boeing's confidence when the company management was getting ready to launch the 367-80 tanker/transport demonstrator program. *Boeing*

Visible on this view of the left wing of the 367-80 are rows of vortex fences, fully deployed spoilers, double-slotted flaps, inboard high-speed ailerons with tabs, and outboard low-speed ailerons. *Boeing*

close beneath the low-mounted and moderately swept wings (an installation not unlike that adopted in the mid-sixties for the Boeing 737), this configuration made possible the use of a conventional tricycle undercarriage. Performance, however, left much to be desired.

Because significant wing sweep was necessary to achieve the desired cruise performance, while at the same time the airlines were expressing a strong preference for low-mounted wings, configuration engineers were frustrated in their attempts to find a satisfactory housing for the main undercarriage units. On the 473-48, for example, the four-wheel main bogies were to retract into pods projecting forward of the leading edge, between the fuselage and the twin-engine pods. On the 473-49B, the main gear consisted of four separate legs, each with a large wheel and retracting forward with the wheel turning 90 degrees to lay flat (a similar but rearward-retracting arrangement had been used by Boeing late during World War II for its XF8B-1 experimental naval fighter). With a satisfactory solution still eluding the project team, the Model 473 came to an inconclusive end shortly after the 473-57 configuration with three J57 turbojets and accommodation for 50 passengers was elaborated in April 1950.

While one Boeing team toiled to come up with a satisfactory Model 473 jetliner configuration, another worked on continued developments of the Model 367 transport and tanker for the USAF. Combining the wings and Wright R-3350 radial engines of the B-29 Superfortress with a double-deck pressurized fuselage, the first of three XC-97 prototypes had flown on

November 9, 1944. Subsequent developments, with more powerful Pratt & Whitney R-4360 radials and B-50 wings and tail surfaces, led to the production of 888 Model 367s as C-97s and KC-97s for the USAF and 56 Model 377 Stratocruisers for airlines. As a tanker, the Model 367 made its debut in 1950 when three C-97As were modified as KC-97A prototypes. Thereafter, no fewer than 811 of the 888 Model 367s were completed as KC-97Es, KC-97Fs, and KC-97Gs. While these numbers reflected the Strategic Air Command's pressing need for tankers in the early Cold War years, they hid the fact that these piston-engined aircraft actually proved marginally satisfactory when refueling B-47 jet bombers.

Substituting turboprops for the radial engines to improve C-97 performance was first contemplated as far back as April 1948 when a 367-15-23 configuration was proposed with Allison T38s, lengthened fuselage of increased diameter, longer span, and a nose-loading ramp. Two months later, the dimensionally larger 367-18-28 configuration was studied with more powerful Allison T40s. Although these design exercises did not result in production configurations, they provided a useful starting point for the 367-23-33 configuration proposed in June 1949 as a boom-equipped tanker with T40 turboprops. The Air Force, however, was not overly concerned by anticipated difficulties of refueling jet bombers with piston-engined tankers.

Work on a turboprop-powered KC-97 was resumed in December 1950 when Boeing attempted to counter the Douglas YKC-124B with its Model 367-60-61 powered by four Pratt & Whitney T34 turboprops and featuring gull wings with 25 degrees of sweep at the quarter chord. During the following month, the 367-64 was proposed with four Pratt & Whitney J57 turbojets as a Navy minelayer or Air Force tanker. Again, Boeing was unsuccessful, but the seed for a jet-powered development of the C-97 had been planted, promising significant performance improvements.

In March 1951, initial B-47 refueling tests with a KC-97A had brought to light the performance shortcoming of piston-engined tankers. As by then Douglas was aggressively marketing its proposed turboprop-powered KC-124B to the Air Force, Boeing put new emphasis on designing turboprop- and turbojet-powered derivatives of its KC-97. These design efforts resulted notably in proposals for the 367-68 with four Bristol Olympus turbojets, the 367-69 with twin J57 pods, the 367-70 with swept wings and Olympus turbojets, the similarly configured 367-71 with J57s, and the 367-77 with four T34 turboprops. Unfortunately for the project team working on advanced developments of the Model 367, in 1951 the Air Force could not yet afford turbine-engined tankers. This may have been a blessing in disguise

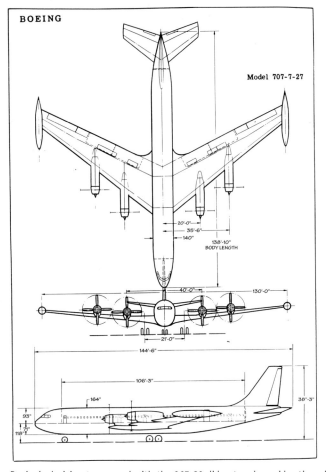

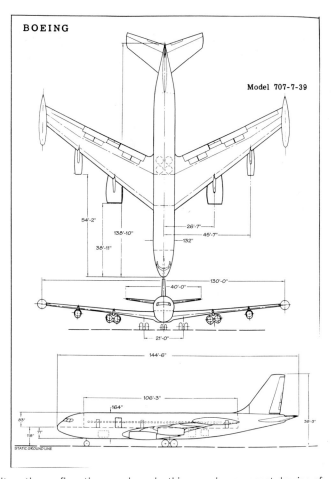

Boeing's decision to proceed with the 367-80 did not end consideration of alternative configurations, as shown by this general arrangement drawing of the turboprop-powered 707-7-27 and of the six-jet 707-7-39. However, these two configurations never reached the hardware stage. *Boeing*

as, until funding for new tankers became likely to be budgeted, Boeing would again concentrate on jetliner designs.

Starting with a clean sheet of paper after earlier Model 473 configurations had failed to result in a satisfactory jetliner design, Boeing launched Model 707 jetliner preliminary design studies in September 1951. From the start, a solution was found for the previously frustrating problem of main undercarriage retraction. With the basic layout now calling for low-mounted wings with 35 degrees of sweep at the quarter chord, the main elements of the tricycle gear would be located close enough to the center of gravity to facilitate rotation on take-off while being placed far enough aft to prevent the tail from coming in contact with the ground during aft loading. Using this arrangement, the 707-1 layout dated November 16, 1951 called for an aircraft providing accommodation for 72 first-class passengers in a 122-inch (3.10-meter) wide cabin and powered by four J57s in twin pods. In the months that followed, the design evolved only slightly, while wing area and fuselage cross section were enlarged.

By the early spring of 1952, engineers finally felt that the 707-6 layout shown on the accompanying three-view drawing was close to what airlines wanted. Intended to be powered by four 9,500 pounds thrust (42.3 kN) civil derivatives of the Pratt & Whitney J57-P-1, the aircraft had wings with span of 130 feet (39.62 meters), area of 2,510 square feet (233.2 square meters), and 35 degrees of sweep at the quarter chord. Its fuselage was 121 feet 3 inches (36.96 meters) long and had a 132-inch (3.35-meter) diameter to accommodate 76 first-class passengers in a four-abreast arrangement and to incorporate an eight-seat aft lounge. Performance promised to be substantially better than that of the de Havilland Comet 1 with which BOAC was about to start jet service.

Most of the initial 367-80 flights were made with A. M. "Tex" Johnston in the left seat and R. L. "Dick" Loesch in the right seat. In this view taken in August 1954, after the eighth flight of the Boeing demonstrator, both wear standard USAF flight gear of the time. *Boeing*

By then, it had also become almost certain that in the relatively near future the Air Force would, at long last, take the plunge and order turbine-powered tankers. The time had come for the Boeing management to take a calculated risk.

## From Paper to Metal

Popular books, television programs, and even some specialized aviation publications have fostered the myth that the 707 jetliner and KC-135 tanker were the miraculous results of "immaculate conception" following a request from William M. Allen, the Boeing president. That was simply not the case.

As we have seen, Boeing had been conducting jetliner conceptual studies since 1946 while, from 1948 on, it also contemplated turbine-powered tanker derivatives of its Model 367. In the spring of 1952, the president and the board of the Seattle manufacturer also had to consider the company's overall competitive position and financial health. On the civil side of the house, activities had come to a grinding halt with the deliveries of the last Model 377 Stratocruiser to BOAC in May 1950. On the military side, the company had experienced several disappointments, especially when the turboprop-powered Model 495 had lost the Air Force 1951 medium transport competition to the Lockheed Model 082/YC-130, and the company suffered a string of failures in fighter competitions. However, these disappointments were more than offset by numerous successes.

Notwithstanding Douglas' attempts to attract Air Force interest in its turboprop-powered KC-124B, Boeing was still getting additional production contracts for piston-engined tankers (the final KC-97G contract being approved by the Air Force in June 1953). The first of 399 B-47B medium jet bombers were about to be delivered to the Strategic Air Command, and additional contracts were confidently expected. The XB-52 prototype of the eight-engine heavy jet bomber had been rolled out on November 29, 1951, 9 1/2 months after a letter contract had been awarded to Boeing for 13 pre-production B-52As, and confidence ran high that the B-52 would become a major production program. Large-scale production of B-52s would also mean that the Air Force would have to order tankers with compatible performance.

Also playing a major part in convincing the Boeing management to undertake the private venture development of a jet tanker/transport demonstrator was the fact that the company financial position had steadily improved since its nadir in the immediate post World War II period.

## Boeing Revenues and Profits

|  | Gross Sales ($ million) | Net Profits ($ million) |
|---|---|---|
| 1946 | 17.1 | (4.9) |
| 1947 | 22.6 | (0.4) |
| 1948 | 127.3 | 1.7 |
| 1949 | 287.0 | 4.4 |
| 1950 | 307.3 | 10.8 |
| 1951 | 337.3 | 7.1 |
| 1952 | 739.0 | 14.1 |
| 1953 | 918.2 | 20.3 |
| 1954 | 1,033.2 | 37.0 |

Flaps and gear down, the 367-80 shows its graceful lines on the occasion of its 1 hour 24 minute maiden flight on July 15, 1954. *Boeing*

In April 1952, William Allen distributed a questionnaire to five of his senior engineering and finance executives (Wellwood Beall, Fred Collins, Fred Laudan, Ed Wells, and John Yeasting) to elicit their comments regarding the feasibility and desirability of proceeding with the design, manufacturing, and testing of a jet tanker/transport demonstrator. Positive answers were received on April 21 and, with confidence boosted by the successful maiden flight of the YB-52 six days earlier, William Allen recommended to the board of directors that the program be initiated. Reacting favorably, board members authorized a $16 million program on April 22, 1952. Ever since, much has been made of the risk taken by the Boeing directors.

True, $16 million in 1952 dollars represented two and one-quarter time the profit realized by Boeing in the preceding year. However, when expressed in 1998 dollars (using the Consumer Price Index to convert then dollars into today's dollars) that amount was $98.7 million, or 56- to 62-percent of the current price of a single 747-400, a not so formidable sum! Moreover, Boeing could expect to charge some of this expenditure to the U.S. government as "Independent Research and Development." It did, in fact, do so when in 1957, under an Air Force contract, the XB-52 was modified by replacing the outboard pairs of J57s by single J75s to help in the development of the JT4A installation for Boeing 707 Models 220 and 320. (Similarly, Douglas got the Navy to pay for the substitution of J75s for J57s in an A3D-1 to test the JT4A installation planned for DC-8 Series 20 and 30.)

When the Board decided to proceed with the 367-80 demonstrator, hopes were high that production military tankers and civil jetliners would be closely related and would be built using similar tooling. This led to protracted negotiations

The initial 144-inch (3.66-meter) cross-section of the 707 was well suited for four-abreast first class seating and five-abreast tourist accommodation (as shown in this photograph of the mock-up—note absence of baggage on the rack above the "passengers" to make room for klieg lights). The need for six-abreast economy class seating forced Boeing to widen the fuselage of its jetliners to "call and raise" the wider Douglas fuselage. *Boeing*

between the Air Force and the manufacturer, as the government sought to recover some of the money apparently spent for the benefit of commercial derivatives. In the end, however, the 707 and the KC-135 only had some 20-percent commonality, as competitive pressures forced Boeing to adopt a wider fuselage cross-section and wings of greater span and area for production 707 models. Moreover, designed for a longer service life, the 707 used 2024 aluminum alloy instead of the lighter 7178 alloy adopted for "shorter-lived" Air Force tankers (something which eventually proved to be a costly mistake, as KC-135s and derivatives will remain in service long after the last 707 jetliners will have been cut by blowtorches of metal smelters).

Although the tanker/transport demonstrator was based on the 707-6 preliminary design layout, it was given the misleading 367-80 designation to make it to appear as being merely a jet derivative of the KC-97 series. (With the benefit of time, one must now wonder how Boeing could seriously expect to succeed with this bit of disinformation—during the 1950s the Soviets were not the sole experts when it came to *disinformatsiya*—as engineers freely moved from Boeing, to Douglas, and then to Lockheed, in search for better jobs. In the process, they took along proprietary information. It is doubtful that Douglas was long fooled into believing that the 367-80 was a mere development of the KC-97 instead of being the all new design it was.) By the time the 367-80 flew in July 1954, all pretenses had been dropped and the aircraft carried the 707 designation on its fin and the N70700 registration number.

By the time the 367-80 was officially announced in September 1952, some three weeks after Douglas had announced its intent to develop a DC-8 jetliner, Boeing had switched from its initially favored twin-engine pods to single-engine pods to meet ATA recommendations. Detailed design also resulted in the adoption of multi-surface flight controls. For control at high speeds, the 367-80 was provided (as were its KC-135 and 707 derivatives) with inboard ailerons between inboard and outboard trailing-edge flaps and four-segment upper-surface spoilers. For control at low speeds, these surfaces were supplemented by outboard ailerons which were locked in neutral position when flaps were up.

Quite surprisingly, the team led by Chief Design Engineer Maynard L. Pennell elected to dispense with servo-hydraulic boost for all primary flying controls (whereas Douglas adopted a dual hydraulic system for its DC-8) in favor of aerodynamically balanced and manually operated controls with spring tabs. Later, however, Boeing adopted powered rudder controls for the 707 and KC-135 and retrofitted the 367-80 with 707 powered-rudder controls in January 1958.

Before manufacturing of the 367-80, a.k.a. 707-7, got much under way, Boeing still evaluated alternative configurations and powerplant installations. Notably, a 707-7-27 configuration dated August 17, 1952 featured wingtip tanks and T34 turbo-props mounted above and forward of the 35-degree swept wings. A few days later, a 707-7-39 configuration retained the wingtip tanks but was to be powered by six J57s in two twin pods and two single pods. Thereafter only minor configuration changes were made as the 367-80 slowly proceeded from concept to reality.

Bearing the Boeing serial number (S/N) 17158 and the Federal Aviation Administration (FAA) registration N70700, the 367-80 demonstrator was completed two weeks ahead of schedule in the Renton plant, on the shores of Lake Washington. Rolled out on May 14, 1954, it was christened "Jet Stratoliner" and "Jet Stratotanker" by Mrs. William E. Boeing, the wife of the company's founder. Flight trials were scheduled to commence shortly afterward but, on May 21, the aircraft was damaged when a main landing gear attachment fitting failed during a taxi test to check the brakes. Investigation revealed that the gear had failed due to secondary loads imposed by deflection. Only moderate damage to the left wingtip and outboard nacelle resulted from this incident, but the gear had to be modified to prevent structural deflections caused by the braking loads.

Comparative cross-sections of the 367-80, the KC-135A (and the initially proposed 707 configuration), and the production standard 707 (and later 727, 737, and 757). *Mark Meredith*

## The Log of the 367-80

Once damage incurred in the taxiing tests had been repaired and the main gear modified, the 367-80 was readied for its first flight. With A. M. "Tex" Johnston in the left seat and R. L. "Dick" Loesch in the right seat and weight limited to 110,000 pounds (49,895 kilograms), the aircraft lifted off at 2:14 P.M. on July 15, 1954 after using only 2,100 feet (640 meters) of the 5,400 foot (1,645 meter) runway in Renton. Lasting 1 hour 24 minutes, the maiden flight saw the aircraft reaching a maximum altitude of 20,000 feet (6,100 meters) with the test crew conducting low- and medium-altitude shakedown, exploring general handling characteristics, evaluating lateral control with flaps extended and retracted, and checking approach stalls.

On July 17, the second flight lasted 2 hours 25 minutes during which similar test activities were complemented by the operation of air conditioning and windshield heating systems. During that flight, the 367-80 was taken to 27,300 feet (8,320 meters) and was flown at 485 miles per hour (780 kilometers per hour) true airspeed. Initial high-altitude shakedown to verify systems and control effectiveness saw the aircraft reaching an altitude of 42,000 feet (12,800 meters) and flying at Mach 0.8 during a 2-hour 19-minute flight on July 17.

On July 20, flights 4 and 5 lasted 2 hours 10 minutes, including a simulated "go-around," during which emergency systems and manual flap extension were evaluated. The next day, the aircraft flew 3 hours and 55 minutes in a program including full-power climb to operational altitude for collection of engine cooling and pressure data, sound level measurement, shutdown and restart of engines at operational altitudes, normal descent at 5,000 and 6,000 feet/minute (25.4 and 30.5 meters/second) with airbrakes extended and gear down, and performance runs with trailing airspeed bomb to calibrate the aircraft-speed measuring system. Flight 7 on July 22, during which the test crew was

primarily tasked with minimum control speed and stall investigations at high altitude, also saw the 367-80 fly briefly in formation with a B-52 to simulate air refueling.

In the course of 15 hours 46 minutes during the first eight days, the 367-80 had demonstrated good flying characteristics and shown that its proposed tanker derivative would have the performance required to refuel the B-52 and other jet bombers. After two weeks in the shop to be readied for the general performance evaluation phase of the test program, the 367-80 again flew on August 5. The 1-hour 4-minute flight went well but, on landing, the brakes got too hot and failed. To avoid overrunning the short runway, Tex Johnston deliberately steered the aircraft onto the dirt on the edge of the runway. The aircraft decelerated rapidly but, before coming to rest, the nose gear collapsed. Repairs were made during the next six weeks with flight tests resuming on September 20. Three days later, the 367-80 made the first series of touch-and-go to evaluate stability and control around the field. On September 24, the aircraft made its longest flight to date, remaining airborne 5 hours and 5 minutes during airspeed calibration with a USAF F-86A Sabre serving as

Faded with time, this early test flight photograph of the 367-80 shows the limited number of cabin windows in the fuselage of this demonstrator. The nacelle housing JT3P turbojets still lack noise suppressors and thrust reversers. *Boeing.*

Although designated 367-80, the jet-powered Boeing tanker/transport demonstrator bore no resemblance with piston-engined Model 367 tankers and transports (the aircraft in the background being KC-97Gs with their distinctive 700-gallon external tanks). Taken on the flying-boat ramp at the Renton plant, this photograph clearly shows the two main-deck cargo doors of the 367-80. *Boeing*

a pacer aircraft. The initial flight test program was completed on September 29, 1954 with the 367-80 having logged 43 hours 27 minutes in 26 flights.

## Technical Data For the Boeing 367-80

**Dimensions:** Span 130 feet (39.62 meters); length overall 127 feet 10 inches (38.96 meters); height 38 feet 3 inches (11.66 meters); fuselage width 11 feet (3.35 meters); fuselage height 13 feet 8 inches (4.17 meters); wheel base 44 feet (13.41 meters); wheel track 21 feet (6.40 meters); wing area 2,400 square feet (222.4 square meters).

**Weights:** Maximum take-off weight 190,000 pounds (86,182 kilograms); operating weight empty 88,890 pounds (40,320 kilograms).

**Powerplant:** Initial installation: four Pratt & Whitney JT3P turbojets with take-off static thrust of 9,500 pounds (42.3 kN) dry or 11,000 pounds (48.9 kN) with water injection at sea level on a standard day (59 degrees Fahrenheit/15° degrees Celsius), and maximum continuous static thrust of 8,250 pounds (36.7 kN).

**Accommodation:** Flight crew of three (pilot, copilot, and flight engineer). Aircraft not fitted out to airline standard but could have accommodated a maximum of 130 passengers in five-abreast configuration.

**Performance:** Maximum speed 478 knots at 35,000 feet (885 kilometers per hour at 10,670 meters); cruising speed 435 knots (805 kilometers per hour); service ceiling 40,000 feet (12,190 meters); maximum range without payload 2,600 nautical miles (4,815 kilometers).

Returned to flight status on October 2, the 367-80 made eight flights on that day: a 33-minute check of spoiler flutter and a 59-minute checkout flight were followed by the first customer demonstration flights for the benefit of Messrs. Gledhill and Kaufman from Pan American World Airways. On October 7, by which time the Air Force had already ordered 117 KC-135As as "interim" jet tankers pending selection of the winner of its KC-X competition, General Albert Boyd became the first USAF officer to be taken aloft in the Boeing tanker demonstrator. The first demonstration to a prospective foreign customer was given on December 2 for BOAC. The year 1954 ended with the 367-80 having logged 92 hours and 30 minutes in 59 flights.

After the holiday break, ground testing resumed on January 7, 1955, and the first flight of the year was made on January 13 when the aircraft was airborne for 35 minutes for a functional test before full resumption of flight tests. During the following months, tests continued at a slightly higher pace than in 1954 as Boeing expanded the 367-80 flight envelope until the middle of June. The aircraft was then returned to the shop to be fitted with a flying boom and air refueling station beneath its rear fuselage. Clearly, the addition of this equipment did not affect handling characteristics negatively as on August 7, 1955, at the end of the second flight in tanker configuration, Tex Johnston slow rolled the 367-80 in front of the crowd during the Gold Cup boating competition on Lake Washington. During the following weeks, Boeing undertook boom flutter, stability, and control tests before the first "dry contact" with a B-52A was made on September 15 during the 367-80's 155th flight.

While still fitted with its flying boom and boom operator station, the 367-80 flew its longest flight ever on October 6 when it was airborne for 5 hours 48 minutes over a Seattle–Denver–Los Angeles–Seattle circuit. The length of this flight is notable as the 187 preceding flights had only averaged 1 hour and 27 minutes while the 1,503 flights that followed before completion of the Boeing flight test program in 1970 averaged 1 hour and 23 minutes.

One week after this long-duration flight, Pan American World Airways announced its historic order for 45 jetliners. The news, however, was not good for Boeing as Pan American

After being modified as a testbed for the Bendix AN/AMQ-15 Weather Reconnaissance System, the 367-80 made 11 flights between April 26 and August 21, 1959 in the configuration shown in this photograph, taken on the ramp at Boeing Field. *Boeing*

November 8 it won an order for 707-123s from American Airlines. On December 24, it prompted Pan American to revise its two-month old order for Boeing jetliners with 144-inch cross-section to include both JT3C- and JT4A-powered 707-121s and -321s with the new standard 148-inch cross-section. After a nasty scare, Boeing was back in the race and testing of the "narrow-body" 367-80 gained tempo in support of the new "wide-body" 707 variants.

While Douglas and Boeing were battling to secure the first orders for American jetliners, the 367-80 got some favorable publicity when it made its first transcontinental flight on October 16, 1955. Eastbound, it flew from Seattle to Andrews AFB, Maryland, in 4 hours 27 minutes while the return trip, benefiting from unusually favorable winds, was made in 4 hours 21 minutes. (Typically, transcontinental westbound flights are 30 minutes to one hour longer than eastbound flights due to prevailing winds from the west.)

As demonstrated again during these transcontinental dashes, the Pratt & Whitney JT3P turbojets initially fitted to the 367-80 were remarkably reliable. However, they were also very noisy. In the late 1950s, airport neighbors were far from being as vociferous as they are today when complaining about noise. Nevertheless, airlines and airport operators shuddered when contemplating what would face them following the introduction of noisy jets at urban airports. These concerns led Boeing to undertake a long and difficult noise attenuation program using jet exhaust suppressor nozzles of its own design or supplied by vendors.

During 1956, the 367-80 logged more flights (237) and more airborne time (284 hours and 29 minutes) than in any previous or later years. With the 707 sales campaign now in full swing, numerous demonstration flights were made during that year for the benefit of initial and prospective civil customers (Air India, American, Aramco, BEA, BOAC, Canadian Pacific, Cubana, LAV, National, Northwest, Pan American, Qantas, SAS, Swissair, Trans Canada, TWA, and VARIG) as well as for the USAF (including the crew of Air Force One) and the U.S. Navy.

ordered only 20 JT3C-powered Boeing 707-121s while signing for 25 JT4A-powered Douglas DC-8-30s.

When Douglas had announced on June 7, 1955 that it would no longer wait for firm orders before going ahead with its JT4A-powered DC-8 jetliner with a fuselage cross-section optimized for six-abreast economy accommodation, Boeing had felt that the slightly wider fuselage of the DC-8 would not be a decisive factor. (Earlier, at the behest of the Air Force, Boeing had already been forced to increase the cross-section of its KC-135 and proposed 707 to 144 inches/3.66 meters—an 8-inch/20.3-centimeter increase over the fuselage cross-section of the 367-80.) Conversely, it realized that the use of more powerful JT4As would enable Douglas to offer a jetliner with better field performance and/or longer range than those of the JT3C-powered 707. Consequently, on September 9, 1955, Boeing had submitted to Pan American detailed specifications for its JT4A-powered 707-221. That proved insufficient to prevent Pan American from favoring the larger and heavier Douglas jetliner. With other carriers also indicating a preference for wider fuselage and more power engines, Boeing quickly issued detailed specifications for JT4A-powered 707 versions with a 148-inch (3.76-meter) cross-section—four inches more than that of the DC-8—specifications for the domestic version being issued on November 1, 1955 and those for the "Intercontinental" version following two weeks later. It was too late to sway United Airlines, which on October 25 ordered DC-8s, but on

In support of the 727 trijet development, the 367-80 was fitted with boundary layer control, leading-edge flaps, and triple-slotted flaps. A JT3C turbojet was mounted on the left side of the rear fuselage to evaluate the proposed rear-mounted JT8D turbofan installation for the 727. The aircraft is seen here at Boeing Field on May 29, 1962 after the rear engine had been replaced by a JT8D-1 fitted with a thrust reverser. *Boeing*

the test program required. Items tested during the year included the fin-tip probe antenna intended for the 707, modified wing leading edges, leading-edge flaps, different types of brakes for the 707 and the KC-135, various vortex generator arrangements atop the wings, autopilots, yaw dampers, antiskid systems, noise suppressors, and cabin soundproofing. Notable flights during 1956 were those on April 20 (when a probe-equipped receiver flew in formation to demonstrate the feasibility of using a boom drogue adapter), on May 9 (when the Dash 80 and a B-47 flew in a simulated refu-

Test activities were undertaken in support of the KC-135A (the first of which flew on August 31, 1956, by which time the 367-80 had logged 547 hours and 47 minutes) and the 707. Consequently, the 367-80 was repeatedly modified during the year with equipment and systems being fitted and removed as

eling formation), and on November 28 (when the nose gear and nose-gear doors jammed during checkout of emergency gear extension; fortunately, after Tex Johnston landed the aircraft hard on its main wheels, the nose gear came down preventing damage to the aircraft).

In support of the Boeing entry in the CX-HLS (C-5) competition for a new USAF heavy logistics aircraft, the 367-80 was fitted with a non-retractable, high-flotation undercarriage with a four-wheel nose gear and eight-wheel main bogies. The aircraft is seen here taxiing on the uneven surface of Harper Dry Lake in California during tests in September 1964. *Boeing*

For the first 9 1/2 months in 1957, flight tests and demonstration flights continued much as in the preceding year but also included evaluation of different thrust reversers. During that period, the 367-80 was also used for a demonstration tour to the East Coast. Departing Seattle on March 11, with a crew and relief crew of 6, the aircraft also carried 32 media representatives, 7 Boeing officials, and 4 Boeing mechanics. Cabin service was provided by three stewardesses from American Airlines, Braniff International Airways, and TWA. The 2,350 miles (3,780 kilometers) between Seattle and the Friendship International Airport in Baltimore, Maryland, were flown in 3 hours 56 minutes, with the aircraft reaching a maximum ground speed of 692 miles per hour (1,113 kilometers per hour). The next day, demonstration flights were flown at Friendship and Andrews AFB for members of Congress, Pentagon officers, the Military Air Transport Service, and more media representatives. On the 14th, the aircraft departed Baltimore with demonstration flights planned in Chicago and Denver (where the aircraft was snowed in, delaying its return to Boeing Field).

Between October 21 and December 19, 1957, the 367-80 was again in the shop for modifications and substitution of a JT4A-3 in the number 2 position (left inboard pod) and a JT3C-4 in the number 3 position to test the powerplant installation of the 707-120 and 707-220/320. The next significant modifications were made in February 1958 (installation of 707-320 fin and boosted rudder), April 1958 (JT3C-6 in lieu of JT3C-4 in the number 3 pod), May 1958 (temporary installation of an icing spray rig ahead of number 3 engine), July 1958 (revised leading-edge flaps), and March 1959 (wing leading-edge extension as devised for the Boeing 720 to reduce drag).

During a lay-up period in April 1959, the 367-80 was modified as a Flying Weather Laboratory under a major cooperative agreement between the Air Force, Navy, Weather Bureau, Boeing, and Bendix Aviation Corp. (which manufactured the AN/AMQ-15 Air Weather Reconnaissance System and headed the industrial team). Modifications included fitting the aircraft with a storm detection radar in an enlarged nose radome; air sampling scoops; conductivity, fair weather, and turbulence wing probes; cloud base and top radar antennas on the rear fuselage; and rocket sonde and drop sonde ejectors. Eleven test flights were made with the AN/AMQ-15 installation between April 26 and August 21 1959. After the Air Weather Reconnaissance System was removed,

Fitted with a nose probe, the JT3D-powered 367-80 is seen here during NASA-Ames variable stability testing at NAS Moffett Field, California, in the spring of 1967. *NASA*

When the 367-80 was refurbished by Boeing prior to being flown for ceremonial hand-over to the National Air and Space Museum in May 1972, its nose probe was removed and the aircraft gained a 707-style radome more pointed than that originally fitted. *Boeing*

the Dash 80 remained grounded until December when five flights were made. By then, with the KC-135A and 707-120 in service, the 367-80 had lost much of its original usefulness.

## In Support of Other Programs

Preliminary work on what would become the 727 trijet had been authorized in May 1958. Among design goals for this short-/medium-range jetliner were improvements in field performance to enable the aircraft to operate from small regional airports and from the 4,860-foot/1,481-meter instrument runway 4-22 at La Guardia Airport in New York. To do so required development and flight testing of advanced high-lift devices and supplementing wind tunnel testing of these devices with flight testing in advance of finalization of the 727 configuration. The availability of the company-owned 367-80 proved fortuitous for Boeing.

To achieve the desired field performance, Boeing engineers initially felt that boundary layer control (BLC) would have to be used on the new aircraft leading- and trailing-edge flaps. Accordingly, the 367-80 was modified during a lay-up period in early 1960, and BLC tests were initiated on February 11. Several flights were then made with main and fillet flaps set at different angles in search of the best stall characteristics. Next, the Dash 80 was fitted with triple-slotted flaps during a lay-up period between November 19, 1960 and February 10, 1961. Two months later, while in that configuration, the aircraft was fitted with a JT3C-6 on the left side of the rear fuselage to test the rear-mounted installation then under consideration for the 727. Still in support of the 727 program, more configuration changes were made in May 1961 (replacement of the dog-leg exhaust pipe of the fuselage-mounted engine by a thrust reverser and addition of

2/9, 1964 after flying 72 hours and 26 minutes with NASA at Langley. First phase of a NASA-Ames variable-stability test program was undertaken in Seattle between July 27 and August 7, 1964. The Dash 80 was then used on August 11/13, 1964 for four dynamic simulation flights in support of the U.S. supersonic transport program.

The Dash 80 also proved useful to Boeing during the Air Force CX-HLS (Cargo Experimental-Heavy Logistics Support) competition which eventually led to the Lockheed C-5. Among design requirements for this heavy cargo jet was the ability to operate from unprepared, or at least semi-prepared, surfaces such as packed snow or sand. Unlike its competitors, Douglas and Lockheed, Boeing elected to demonstrate the feasibility of operations from such surfaces by modifying the 367-80 once again. The nose gear was modified to take four wheels while each main gear leg supported eight-wheel bogies to reduce the footprint of the aircraft, but doubling the number of wheels necessitated lock-

Successful development of the 367-80 led to the production of 724 Model 707s for civil customers (including this 707-430 for Lufthansa German Airline), 129 Model 707s for government and military customers (including E-3 and E-6 variants), and 154 Model 720s. *Boeing*

a heat shield on the left stabilizer), in July/August (full span leading-edge flaps with boundary layer control), between November 1961 and January 1962 (substitution of Pratt & Whitney JT3D-1 turbofans for the mix of main engines and installation of 727 cabin pressurization), in February 1962 (727 wing gear doors), in March 1962 (727 leading-edge slats and Autonetics automatic approach system), in April 1962 (aft-mounted JT3C replaced by a Pratt & Whitney JT8D-1 turbofan). For the most part, the required 727 tests were completed by July 2, 1962 with the Dash 80 having added 293 hours since that program had started 2 1/2 years earlier.

After the rear engine and consigned equipment were removed in July 1962, the Dash 80 was placed in storage for four months until needed for a joint research program with NASA. To that end, it was fitted with wing leading-edge flaps, enlarged blown trailing-edge flaps, and 707-320 horizontal tail surfaces with inverted Krüger flaps on their leading-edge during a lay-up period at the end of 1962. Tests progressed slowly and attachment of the boundary layer was achieved to a flap angle of 80 degrees only on February 25, 1964 after 20 flights in this configuration. The aircraft then remained in Seattle until April 24/26, 1964 when it was ferried to Langley, Virginia, for NASA Phase II testing. It returned to Seattle on July

ing the undercarriage in the down position. High-flotation landing gear tests were initiated in Seattle on September 8, 1964, and, the next day, the aircraft was ferried to Edwards AFB, California, for a three-day test program including operations from the sandy surface of nearby Harper Dry Lake. The Dash 80 again departed Seattle on September 27 for a 12-day demonstration tour taking it in short-distance hops, due to the drag of its non-retractable high-flotation landing gear, to Spokane, Washington; Billings, Montana; Denver, Colorado; Kansas City, Missouri; Dayton, Ohio; Andrews AFB, Maryland; Dulles International Airport, Virginia, where the aircraft was taxied onto the grass; Wright-Patterson AFB, Ohio, where the aircraft took-off and landed in the grass; Pope AFB, North Carolina; Nashville, Tennessee; Scott AFB, Illinois, again taking-off and landing in the grass; Omaha, Nebraska; and back to Seattle with stops in Denver, Billings, and Spokane. The high-flotation gear was removed on October 14, 1964.

In preparation for further variable-stability testing, the 367-80 was next fitted with hydraulically controlled ailerons and elevators and with a nose boom. Tests resumed on January 19, 1965, and three months later the modified 367-80 flew simulations for the Boeing 2707 and Boeing C-5 projects. In May 1965, variable stability demonstrations were flown for

## 367-80 Flight Test Program

| Year | Number of Flights | Cumulative Number of Flights | Flight Hours | Cumulative Number of Flight Hours |
|------|-------------------|------------------------------|--------------|-----------------------------------|
| 1954 | 59 | 59 | 92 hours 30 minutes | 92 hours 30 minutes |
| 1955 | 222 | 281 | 268 hours 29 minutes | 360 hours 59 minutes |
| 1956 | 237 | 518 | 284 hours 5 minutes | 645 hours 4 minutes |
| 1957 | 116 | 634 | 155 hours 33 minutes | 800 hours 37 minutes |
| 1958 | 182 | 816 | 326 hours 48 minutes | 1,127 hours 25 minutes |
| 1959 | 47 | 863 | 93 hours 56 minutes | 1,221 hours 21 minutes |
| 1960 | 104 | 967 | 109 hours 46 minutes | 1,331 hours 7 minutes |
| 1961 | 140 | 1,107 | 121 hours 45 minutes | 1,452 hours 52 minutes |
| 1962 | 49 | 1,156 | 61 hours 29 minutes | 1,514 hours 21 minutes |
| 1963 | 4 | 1,160 | 6 hours 3 minutes | 1,520 hours 24 minutes |
| 1964 | 186 | 1,346 | 259 hours 55 minutes | 1,780 hours 19 minutes |
| 1965 | 188 | 1,534 | 275 hours 26 minutes | 2,055 hours 45 minutes |
| 1966 | 0 | 1,534 | 0 | 2,055 hours 45 minutes |
| 1967 | 32 | 1,566 | 59 hours 21 minutes | 2,115 hours 6 minutes |
| 1968 | 69 | 1,635 | 130 hours 2 minutes | 2,245 hours 8 minutes |
| 1969 | 51 | 1,686 | 99 hours 22 minutes | 2,344 hours 30 minutes |
| 1970 | 5 | 1,691 | 5 hours 16 minutes | 2,349 hours 46 minutes |

NASA-Ames on the 4th, NASA-Langley on the 6th, the Air Force Flight Test Center on the 7th, and the Cornell Aeronautical Laboratories on the 8th. Further testing under NASA contract was then undertaken in Seattle before the aircraft was flown to NASA-Langley, Virginia, between July 6 and 9, 1965, via Great Falls, Montana; Casper, Wyoming; Kansas City, Missouri; and Nashville, Tennessee. Remaining in Virginia until October 11, the aircraft accumulated 106 hours and 27 minutes during NASA-Langley evaluation. It next was prepared for a Large Transport evaluation by NASA-Ames during which it flew 25 hours and 49 minutes while temporarily based at NAS Moffett Field, California. Ferried back from California on December 15, 1965, the 367-80 then remained idle at Boeing Field until April 14, 1967.

Again needed by NASA-Ames for a follow-on Large Transport and supersonic transport aircraft (SST) simulation program, the aircraft returned to Naval Air Station (NAS) Moffett Field on April 28, 1967. After flying 43 hours and 36 minutes while with Ames, the 367-80 was ferried to Kansas for use by Boeing Wichita (WIBAC) in support of boundary layer control and automatic-landing tests. While with WIBAC, 156 hours and 8 minutes were logged before the aircraft was returned to Seattle. A final period with the Seattle Flight Test Organization during which advanced automatic landing systems were evaluated brought the log total to 2,349 hours and 46 minutes in 1,691 flights. The last of these flights was made on January 22,

1970 on the occasion of a Space Shuttle Symposium at Payne Field, Washington.

## In Limbo

Donated to the National Air and Space Museum, Smithsonian Institution, the 367-80 was flown to Dulles International Airport, Virginia, on May 26, 1972 for a ceremonial transfer. However, as the National Air and Space Museum would not have adequate display space for such a large aircraft until completion of its facility at the Dulles International Airport, the Dash 80 was flown the next day to Davis-Monthan AFB, Arizona, for safe keeping in the Military Aircraft Storage & Disposition Center. Given the MASDC (later AMARC) inventory number CA006, the veteran tanker/jetliner demonstrator and flying laboratory remained in the Arizona desert for 18 years.

On loan from the National Air and Space Museum, still without its long-awaited Dulles facility, the 367-80 was ferried back to Seattle on May 7, 1990. After refurbishing by the manufacturer, the Dash 80 made a special fly-over of the five Boeing facilities on July 15, 1991, to celebrate the 75th anniversary of the Boeing Company. After its JT3D-1s were shut off for the last time at the end of a final flight on August 29, 1991, the 367-80 had logged 2,373 hours and 21 minutes.

Now stored at Boeing Field, the historical aircraft awaits the day when the Smithsonian Institution will, at long last, give it the shrine it deserves.

# CHAPTER TWO
## GROWING FAMILY

Anticipating that an order for jet tankers would be both easier to secure and larger, Boeing had given priority to developing tanker variants of the 367-80 demonstrator. The soundness of this decision became evident when an Air Force Procurement Authorization for 29 KC-135As was announced on August 6, 1954, barely three weeks after the maiden flight of the 367-80 and only 15 days after the tanker/transport demonstrator had first performed a simulated air refueling of a Boeing B-52. Additional KC-135A orders received on August 27, 1954 (for 88 aircraft) and in February 1955 (for 169 aircraft) further vindicated

the decision to secure military orders before seeking airline contracts. However, hopes to convert quickly the military selection of the Boeing tanker into orders from the leading airlines were frustrated by the caution which carriers showed toward jetliners following the tragic and untimely demise of the de Havilland Comet 1.

Less than six months after entering service with British Overseas Airways Corporation, the first Comet 1 had been damaged beyond economical repair in a take-off accident in Rome, Italy. Over the next 17 months, five more of the 17 Comet 1s were lost, the last two disintegrating in flight and prompting the grounding of the pioneering British jetliner. Alarmed, airlines adopted a "wait-and-see" attitude pending results from a thorough accident investigation by the Royal Aircraft Establishment at Farnborough.

Notwithstanding this cautionary approach on the part of the major carriers, Boeing appeared to have an unbeatable lead, as by February 1955 it could boast Air Force contracts for no fewer than 286 KC-135As. However, unwilling to concede its 20-year lead as the world's foremost manufacturer of medium- and long-range airliners, the Douglas Aircraft Company decided to challenge Boeing. On June 7, 1955, before Boeing was able to secure an order for its jetliner, Douglas confirmed that it would proceed with the development of a jet transport with performance surpassing that of the first Boeing 707 civil derivative of the 367-80 demonstrator.

Yet to receive their Pan American livery, the third (S/N 17588, N709PA) and first (S/N 17586, N708PA) 707-121s pose for a Boeing photographer on May 16, 1958, one day after N709PA had made its first flight. *Boeing*

Built for American Airlines as a 707-123B, S/N 19335 was acquired by Omega Air Inc. in October 1989 and was subsequently leased by them to several carriers. It is seen here landing at the Miami International Airport in March 1992 while on lease to Aeronica as YN-CDE. *Kevin Cook*

To counter the Convair 880, Boeing developed the 720 as a lower capacity derivative of the 707-120. N8702E is shown in the old Eastern Air markings in which it was delivered to this Miami-based carrier. *Boeing*

El Al, the Israeli flag carrier, first ordered two 707-458s in March 1960. The first of these Conway-powered aircraft, 4X-ATA *Shehecheyanu*, was delivered on April 22, 1961. *Boeing*

The Douglas challenge was made even more dangerous for Boeing by the fact that the Southern California manufacturer had an intimate knowledge of what airlines needed as it had successfully developed its pre-war–designed, unpressurized DC-4 into the pressurized DC-6 and DC-7 series with ever increasing speed, range, and payload. Commercially, DC-4s had first been used by American Export Airlines in October 1945 to provide a multi-stop transatlantic service between New York and England. Next, the DC-6 had been used by United Airlines to initiate single-stop service between the West Coast and New York in April 1947. This was followed in May 1952 by Pan American's introduction of tourist class service over the North Atlantic with DC-6Bs. On the prime U.S. transcontinental route, the DC-7 enabled American Airlines to begin nonstop coast-to-coast service in November 1953. Twenty-one months later, Pan American was able to commence nonstop eastbound service between New York and Europe with the DC-7B while planning to start nonstop westbound service—an undertaking made more challenging by prevailing headwinds—during the following year with the even longer-ranged DC-7C.

Capitalizing on this experience, Douglas designed its DC-8 jetliner to outperform the initial 707 variant marketed by Boeing. In particular, Douglas adopted a wider fuselage cross-section in order to increase seat width in first class and, more importantly, to offer better than simply Spartan six-

abreast seating in economy class versus the five-abreast seating offered by Boeing. Moreover, Douglas was quick to realize that airlines competing over the "Blue Ribbon" North Atlantic route would want to offer nonstop jet service, as multi-stop jet service would only be marginally faster than nonstop piston-engine DC-7C service.

Just as Douglas was unwilling to give up its leading position in the medium- to long-range market, Convair, the dominant American manufacturer of short- to medium-range airliners, was intent on challenging Boeing's lead by developing jetliners optimized for U.S. domestic and shorter international routes. Choosing not to compete with Boeing or Douglas in terms of seating requirements, Convair felt that a cruising speed higher than offered by either the 707 or DC-8 would be the key to success. Accordingly, in January 1956, the San Diego manufacturer announced that it would proceed with the development of its Model 22 Skylark, a jetliner slightly smaller but faster than the Boeing 707.

With the initial configurations of its 707 challenged at the lower end of the market by the smaller and faster Convair 880 and its turbofan-powered derivative, the Convair 990, and at the upper end of the market by the larger, heavier, and roomier Douglas DC-8 variants, Boeing was quickly forced to depart from its original intent to offer the 707 only in long-body and short-body versions powered by JT3C turbojets. To meet the Douglas challenge, it was forced to offer larger and heavier

JT4A turbojet-powered and Conway and JT3D turbofan-powered 707 models; at the same time, it addressed the Convair challenge with smaller and lighter 720 variants. In addition, in then-unsuccessful attempts to regain the initiative, Boeing studied still larger and heavier variants, but none of them went into production.

Rather than describing 707 and 720 variants in the traditional sequential order based on model designations, these variants are detailed hereafter in calendar order based on design dates to record more logically the development chronology of the first Boeing jetliners.

## 707-120

Dated November 16, 1951, layout drawings for the first design to bear a Model 707 designation show an aircraft with 35 degrees of wing sweep and four J57 engines in twin-podded nacelles, one under each wing. Intended to accommodate 72 first-class passengers, this 707-1 had a fuselage width of only 122 inches (3.10 meters), slightly less than featured by the most successful contemporary propliners, the Douglas DC-6/DC-7 series, the fuselage of which had a constant width of 125 inches (3.18 meters). This shortcoming was corrected with the 707-2 layout which provided for a fuselage width of 132 inches (3.35 meters). Although still less than the 139.3-inch (3.54-meter) maximum fuselage width of the Lockheed Constellation/Super Constellation propliner series, the 132-inch width was that of the upper deck of the Boeing 377 Stratocruiser, a propliner offering first-class accommodation in a four-abreast seating arrangement praised by passengers. Accordingly, this width was retained for the 367-80 and its intended 707-7 production jetliner version until the Air Force concluded that it would not provide enough clearance for efficient loading and carriage of standard military pallets on the upper deck.

In the meanwhile, mockups of airliner cabins had shown that a 144-inch (3.66-meter) fuselage diameter would not only provide for increased comfort in four-abreast first-class seating but would also work for five-abreast tourist-class and six-abreast economy-class accommodations. Therefore, Boeing increased the diameter of its proposed Model 717 tanker and 707 jetliners to 144 inches before negotiations with airlines began in earnest. That width was found acceptable to the first commercial customer, since Pan American was initially interested in the 707 only as a temporary aircraft that would enable it to match the anticipated introduction of transatlantic jet service by BOAC with de Havilland Comet 4s while waiting to build up its jetliner fleet with the larger, heavier, and more powerful Douglas DC-8.

Unfortunately for Boeing, because domestic trunk carriers did not face the competitive threat of Comet 4 operators, they did not plan on ordering two types of medium- to long-range jetliners as Pan American

| Model | FAA Type Certificate | First Flight | First Delivery | First Service |
|---|---|---|---|---|
| 367-80 | Not certificated | Jul 15, 1954 | Not delivered | N/A |
| 707-120 | 4A21 Sep 10, 1958 | Dec 20, 1957 | Aug 15, 1958 | Oct 26, 1958 |
| 707-120B | Addendum to 4A21 Mar 1, 1961 | Jun 22, 1960 | May 25, 1961 | Jun 11, 1961 |
| 707-220 | Addendum to 4A21 Nov 5, 1959 | May 11, 1959 | Dec 3, 1959 | Dec 20, 1959 |
| 707-320 | 4A26 Jul 15, 1959 | Jan 11, 1958 | Aug 20, 1958 | Aug 26, 1959 |
| 707-320B | Addendum to 4A26 May 31, 1962 | Jan 31, 1962 | Apr 12, 1962 | Jun 1, 1962 |
| 707-320C | Addendum to 4A26 Apr 30, 1963 | Feb 19, 1963 | May 2, 1963 | Jun 3, 1963 |
| 707-420 | Addendum to 4A26 Feb 12, 1960 | May 19, 1959 | Apr 28, 1960 | May 27, 1960 |
| 720 | 4A28 Jun 30, 1960 | Nov 23, 1959 | Apr 30, 1960 | Jul 5, 1960 |
| 720B | Addendum to 4A28 Mar 3, 1961 | Oct 6, 1960 | Feb 3, 1961 | Mar 12, 1961 |

S/N 17588, the third 707-121, during a pre-certification flight. On August 15, 1958, this aircraft became the first to be delivered to Pan American. It was lost in an accident near Elkton, Maryland, on December 8, 1963. *Boeing*

had just done. Seeing merits in Douglas' arguments that the 147-inch (3.73-meter) fuselage width of its proposed DC-8 would provide for improved six-abreast economy accommodation, United Airlines selected the Douglas jetliner in preference to the 707 when in October 1955 it became the second carrier to order U.S. jetliners. In spite of the gamble it had taken with the private-venture development of its 367-80 jet transport demonstrator, Boeing was threatened with seeing its efforts frustrated by Douglas' superior understanding of airline requirements. The time had come for a painful reassessment by the management of the Seattle firm.

The perennial competition between American Airlines, United Airlines, and Trans World Airlines on U.S. transcontinental routes provided Boeing with a timely opportunity of regaining the initiative. To be the first to offer jet service across the United States, American favored the 707 over the DC-8 but wanted jetliners offering the best possible accommodation in all classes of service. Putting pressure on Boeing, American

Airlines got the Seattle manufacturer to increase the fuselage width of its 707 to 148 inches (3.76 meters), 1 inch (2.54 centimeter) better than the DC-8 and 15 inches (0.38 meters) more than the Comet 4.

The wider fuselage was quickly adopted as the new Boeing standard, with specifications for the aircraft previously ordered by Pan American being changed accordingly. Significantly, it has been carried forward into the Boeing 727 trijet (first flown in February 1963), the Boeing 737 twinjet (first flown in April 1967), and the Boeing 757 twinjet (first flown in January 1982).

The initial order for JT3C-powered 707s was announced on October 13, 1955 when news of a 20-aircraft order (S/Ns 17586–17605) placed by Pan American was released. This Pan American contract for aircraft with 144-inch fuselage width was later amended to cover aircraft with 148-inch fuselage width. Moreover, Pan American subsequently elected in December 1955 to take only six aircraft as JT3C-powered 707-121s while the balance of the original 20-aircraft order was switched to JT4A-powered 707-321s. The first Pan American-ordered 707-121 (S/N 17586, N708PA) flew on December 20, 1957, and the airline took delivery of its first jetliner (S/N 17588, N709PA) on August 15, 1958. Certification was obtained on September 18, 1958, and scheduled passenger operations commenced on October 26, 1958.

Proposals tailored to specific airline requirements were initially given sequential model numbers starting with 707-121, as first given to the JT3C-powered aircraft ordered by Pan American with 144-inch fuselage but delivered with 148-inch fuselage. The 707-122 designation at first identified the version proposed unsuccessfully to United Airlines with JT3C engines and 144-inch fuselage. The 707-222 and 707-322 designations then briefly identified aircraft proposed to Scandinavian Airlines System respectively with JT3C and JT4A engines. How-

The initial cockpit configuration of the 707 was remarkably uncluttered compared to that of piston-engined aircraft it replaced beginning in 1958. The scope for the weather radar figures prominently on the T console between the seats for the captain and first officer. *Boeing*

ever, in January 1955 Boeing adopted a policy, still in force more than four decades later, whereby the second and third digits of the dash number identified permanently aircraft proposed or built for a given airline. Thus, ever since, the last two "21" designation digits have identified aircraft for Pan American (such as the 707-121/-321/-321B/321C, 727-21/-21QC/-221, 747-121/-221F, and 741SP-21). The "22" Customer Modified Series Number, to use the proper Boeing moniker for such designators, has been given to aircraft for United Airlines (such as the 720-022). Similarly, "23" designations have identified aircraft for American Airlines (such as the 767-223) while "24" designations specified aircraft for Continental Airlines (such as the 727-224), etc.

In addition to JT3C-powered aircraft with the standard 138 foot 10 inch (42.32 meter) long-body, Boeing offered a short-body version (with 10 feet/3.05 meters being removed aft of the wings to reduce fuselage length to 128 feet 10 inches/39.27 meters) tailored for overwater service. Powered by four JT3C-6 engines and fitted with center-section fuel tanks to increase fuel

capacity from the basic 13,486 U.S. gallons/51,049 liters to 17,286 gallons/65,433 liters, this "short body" variant first appeared in a 120B layout drawing dated September 7, 1956. The only airline to avail itself of the greater range of this version was Qantas Airlines, as the Australian carrier had, first, to contend with what then were unusually long overwater sectors (such the 2,080-nautical mile/3,853-kilometer still-air distance San Francisco–Honolulu leg, the 2,269-nautical mile/4,203-kilometer Honolulu–Pago Pago sector, and the 2,375-nautical mile/4,399-kilometer Pago Pago–Sydney hop) and second, to navigate these sectors without suitable diversionary jet airfields. The first 707-138 (S/N 17696 as N31239 but later delivered as VH-EBA) flew on March 20, 1959 and deliveries to Qantas began on June 26, 1959. The seven 707-138s built for the Australian carrier became the first 707s certificated to carry a spare engine in a pod mounted under the left wing inboard of the number 2 engine.

Early production long-and short-body 707-120s were delivered with the so-called "short" vertical-tail surfaces and

The only customer for the short-body 707 was Qantas, Australia's overseas airline. With its water-injected JT3Cs roaring and belching up smoke, this aircraft takes off with a pod for a spare engine mounted between the number 2 engine and the fuselage. *Boeing*

manually operated rudder. However, as the result of modifications developed to obtain British certification of the 707-420 series, the fin was extended upward, the rudder was provided with hydraulic boost, and, in most instances, a ventral fin was added to improve handling in asymmetric engine conditions. These modifications were incorporated during production in late 1959, and most early production aircraft were retrofitted. The ventral fin, which was not always fitted or retrofitted, also helped to prevent the rear fuselage from hitting the runway during excessive rotation on take-off. Another modification had been retrofitted to the first 707-121s aircraft before they were delivered to Pan American and was incorporated early on during production. This modification, which consisted of fitting two segments of Krüger-type leading-edge flaps inboard of the number 1 and 4 engines, delayed wing stall at slow speeds when deployed at the same time as the double-slotted trailing-edge flaps.

Known as 707-120s under the Boeing designation system, and briefly publicized as the "Jet Stratoliner," but designated 707-100s in the FAA Approved Type Certificate 4A-21 (ATC 4A21) issued on September 18, 1958, 60 JT3C-powered 707s were built for airline customers including 6 707-121s for Pan American, 25 123s for American, 5 124s for Continental, 15 131s for TWA, 7 138s for Qantas, and 2 139s ordered by Cubana but delivered to Western. In addition, 3 707-153s were delivered to the USAF as VC-137As. Structural differences between models were limited to the size and capacity of the center fuel tank and to localized structural strengthening for models certificated for operations at higher weights. In addition, models differed in cockpit arrangements, avionics, and cabin layout and furnishing as specified by each customer. Thirty-nine of these aircraft, including the three USAF VIP aircraft, were subsequently re-engined with JT3D turbofans as 707-120Bs.

Between August 15, 1959, when S/N 17641 became the first Boeing jetliner lost in an accident, and December 12, 1981, when S/N 17610 was damaged beyond repair in a landing accident, 13 JT3C-powered 707-120s were lost. As of June 30, 1998, the only JT3C-powered 707-120 still carried by Boeing in its listing of active aircraft was S/N 17612 registered 4X-JYE in Israel. Built as a 707-124 and delivered to Continental Airlines in August 1959, this aircraft was subsequently acquired by TWA in December 1967, and by Israel Aircraft Industries on behalf of the Israeli Air Force in November 1971. Although still included in Boeings' active aircraft list, 4X-JYE is believed to have been withdrawn from use in January 1984 and is currently stored at Lod Air Base, the military side of the Ben Gurion International Airport in Tel Aviv.

## Technical Data For the Long-Body Boeing 707-120

**Dimensions:** Span 130 feet 10 inches (39.88 meters); length overall 145 feet 1 inch (44.22 meters); fuselage length 138 feet 10 inches (42.32 meters); height 38 feet 8 inches (11.79 meters) with original fin or 42 feet (12.80 meters) with extended fin; fuselage width 12 feet 4 inches (3.76 meters); fuselage height 14 feet 2.5 inches (4.33 meters); wheel base 52 feet 4 inches (15.95 meters); wheel track 22 feet 1 inch (6.73 meters); wing area 2,433 square feet (226 square meters).

**Weights:** Maximum typical ramp weight 248,000 pounds (112,491 kilograms); maximum optional ramp weight 258,000 pounds (117,027 kilograms); maximum typical take-off weight 246,000 pounds (111,584 kilograms); maximum optional take-off weight 256,000 pounds (116,120 kilograms); maximum landing weight 190,000 pounds (86,183 kilograms); maximum zero fuel weight 170,000 pounds (77,111 kilograms); operating weight empty 118,000 pounds (53,524 kilograms); maximum structural payload 44,400 pounds (20,140 kilograms).

**Powerplant:** Four Pratt & Whitney JT3C-6 turbojets with take-off static thrust of 11,200 pounds (49.8 kN) dry or 13,000 pounds (57.8 kN) with water injection at sea level on a standard day (59 degrees Fahreheit/15 degrees Celsius), and maximum continuous static thrust of 10,000 pounds (44.5 kN). Some engines were later upgraded to the JT3C-6 Advanced standard with take-off thrust with water injection increased to 13,500 pounds (60 kN). Fuel-tank capacity differed according to customer specifications; typical capacity 13,486 U.S. gallons (51,049 liters); maximum optional capacity 17,406 U.S. gallons (65,887 liters).

**Accommodation:** Flight crew of three (captain, first officer, and second officer). Maximum seating for 165 passengers, or 179 passengers if aircraft equipped with four inflatable escape chutes. Typical mixed-class seating for 137 passengers (32 F + 105 Y). Maximum belly cargo volume 1,668 cubic feet (47.3 cubic meters).

**Performance:** Never-exceed speed $V_{ne}$ 385 knots (713 kilometers per hour) or $M_{ne}$ 0.895 Mach; maximum operating speed $V_{mo}$ 339 knots (628 kilometers per hour) at sea level and 377 knots (698 kilometers per hour) at 24,900 feet (7,590 meters) or $M_{mo}$ 0.884 at or above 24,900 feet (7,590 meters); Federal Aviation Regulations (FAR) runway length on a standard day + 15 degrees Celsius (86 degrees Fahrenheit/30° degrees Celsius) 10,700 feet (3,260 meters); FAR landing runway length on a standard day (59 degrees Fahrenheit/15 degrees Celsius) and dry runway 6,450 feet (1,965 meters); range with full payload 2,465 nautical miles (4,565 kilometers); range with full mixed-class passengers and bags 3,310 nautical miles (6,130 kilometers); maximum range without payload 4,040 nautical miles (7,480 kilometers).

**NOTE:** Speed data included in this and subsequent data sheets have been extracted from relevant FAA *Type Certificate Data Sheets*. Airfield performance and payload/range data come from various editions of the *Review of the Boeing Jet Family, Comparative Performance and Operating Costs*.

## 707-320

Having successfully countered the first of Douglas inroads by widening the fuselage of its 707, Boeing still had to meet the challenge of the more powerful, heavier, and longer-ranged JT4A-powered version of the Douglas jetliner. Accordingly, keen on having Pan American move away from its initial preference for the Douglas jet transport, the Seattle manufacturer quickly proposed a JT4A-powered version of its jetliner with wings of increased span and area.

To achieve the desired nonstop transatlantic capability without a payload penalty, not just between European capitals relatively close to the eastern shores of the Atlantic (such as London, Madrid, or Paris) and U.S. or Canadian cities near the western shores (such as Boston, Montreal, or New York) but also from major metropolises further inland (such as Chicago, Frankfurt, Rome, and Zurich), required increases in fuel load and take-off weight. The distances between inland cities is substantially further than distances between coastal cities; for example, London–New York, uncorrected for winds, is only 3,005 nautical miles (5,564 kilometers) whereas Rome–Chicago is 4,176 nautical miles (7,734 kilometers). Heavier take-off weights meant that to avoid downgrading airfield performance excessively, both power and wing area had to be increased while additional high-lift devices had to be provided.

The switch to Pratt & Whitney JT4A turbojets with dry take-off thrust 17- to 35-percent greater than the wet thrust (i.e., using the cumbersome and noisy water injection system) of JT3C variants went a long way to keep take-off field length requirements within reason. Nevertheless, Boeing still needed to redesign the wings to increase area and provide space for additional fuel. This was accomplished by reducing trailing edge sweep between the wing fillet and the inboard engines and by extending the outboard panels to increase span from 130 feet 10 inches to 142 feet 5 inches (39.88 to 43.41 meters) and

Parallel production lines for Air Force KC-135s and civil 707-120s at the Renton plant on July 31, 1958. The aircraft in the foreground is a 707-123 for American Airlines. *Boeing*

length requirements some 12 percent greater than a fully loaded 707-120.

The 707-320 retained the newly adopted 148-inch fuselage diameter, but cabin length, from the cockpit door to the rear pressure bulkhead, was increased 6 feet 8 inches (2.03 meters) to 111 feet 6 inches (33.99 meters). Standard seating was increased from 96 to 104 first-class passengers with 40-inch (1.02-meter) seat pitch and from 165 to 180 economy-class passengers with 34-inch (0.86-meter) seat pitch. With special seats and inflatable escape hatches, the 707-320 was certificated to carry a maximum of 189 passengers in high-density configuration. Other structural changes included a strengthened undercarriage, stronger skin panels, and larger horizontal tail surfaces (with span increased from 39 feet 8 inches to 45 feet 8 inches/12.09 meters to 13.92 meters).

area from 2,433 to 2,892 square feet (226 to 268.7 square meters). The larger wings, however, retained the 35 degree of sweep at the quarter chord and two-spar structure of the original 367-80 wings. A collateral benefit from enlarging the wings was a reduction in cabin noise as the engines were moved further outboard, the centerline of the inboard JT4As of the -320 being 33 feet (10.06 meters) from the fuselage centerline, whereas that distance was only 27 feet 2 inches (8.28 meters) in the case of the inboard JT3C of the -120.

To increase lift, the larger wings were fitted with split fillet flaps on the trailing-edge between the fuselage and the inboard sections of double-slotted flaps and two additional sections of Krüger-type flaps on the leading-edge. This revised configuration enabled approach speed to be reduced from 145 knots (269 kilometers per hour) for the 707-120 to 140 knots (260 kilometers per hour) for the -320 in spite of the greater weight of the latter. Notwithstanding the use of more powerful engines and larger wings, however, the heavier 707-320 (with a maximum gross take-off weight between 18 and 28 percent greater than the 707-120 depending on configuration) still ended up having Federal Aviation Regulations (FAR) runway

Briefly marketed under the "Intercontinental" name, the 707-320 was first ordered by Pan American on December 24, 1955 when the original 707 customer amended its contract for 20 aircraft to cover 6 JT3C-powered 707-121s and 14 JT4A-powered 707-321s. Quickly, several international carriers in the United States and abroad followed suit, with the French and Belgian national flag carriers becoming the first 707 foreign customers when on December 28, 1955 they respectively ordered 10 707-328s and 4 707-329s.

The first of the larger and heavier models flew on January 11, 1959, and the 707-321 was placed in service by Pan American on August 26, 1959. Although rapidly supplanted by its turbofan-powered derivatives (the 707-420, 707-320B, and 707-320C), the JT4A-powered intercontinental version of the 707 sold better than the original JT3C-powered variant. Altogether 69 were built, including 20 707-321s for Pan American, 21 -328s for Air France, 7 -329s for Sabena, 12 -331s for TWA, 6 -331s ordered by TWA but delivered to Pan American, and 3 -344s for South African Airways. Initial deliveries were with "short" fin and manually operated

Built in the Boeing Transport Division factory at Renton, 707s had to be towed across the Cedar River bridge to the Renton Municipal Airport from where all were first flown. The fourth 707-124 for Continental Airlines is fitted with the original short vertical surfaces. *Boeing, courtesy of Peter M. Bowers*

rudder, but most -320 series aircraft were delivered with the larger surfaces and hydraulically boosted rudder. Aircraft delivered in the early configuration were retrofitted. According to their need, airlines specified different models of the JT4A turbojet with take-off thrust of 15,800 pounds (70.3 kN) for the JT4A-3 and -5, 16,800 pounds (74.7 kN) for the -9, and 17,500 pounds (77.8 kN) for the -11 and -12 models.

Seven 707-320s (or 707-300s according to the FAA-favored designation used in the ATC 4A26) were destroyed in flying accidents between January 15, 1961, when S/N 17624, a 707-329 of Sabena, crashed on approach to Brussels National Airport in Belgium, and December 20, 1980, when S/N 17605, a former Pan American 707-321 then operated by Aerotal Colombia, burnt at the Aeropuerto de El Dorado in Bogota, Colombia, following a heavy landing. Another aircraft, S/N 17620, a 707-328 of Air France, was destroyed at the Ajaccio-Campo dell'Oro Airport when a bomb planted by Corsican terrorists exploded on the ground.

As of June 30, 1998, Boeing still included eight 707-320s in its list of active aircraft. However, none of the seven noisy JT4A-powered registered in Israel have been flown much in recent years, while the General Electric CFM56 testbed, an ex-Pan American 707-321, is inactive at the Mojave Airport in California.

## Technical Data For the Boeing 707-320

**Dimensions:** Span 142 feet 5 inches (43.41 meters); length overall 152 feet 11 inches (46.61 meters); fuselage length 145 feet 6 inches (44.35 meters); height 41 feet 8 inches (12.70 meters); fuselage width 12 feet 4 inches (3.76 meters); fuselage height 14 feet 2.5 inches (4.33 meters); wheel base 59 feet (17.98 meters); wheel track 22 feet 1 inch (6.73 meters); wing area 2,892 square feet (268.7 square meters).

**Weights:** Maximum typical ramp weight 302,000 pounds

The name "Intercontinental," as seen applied on the first JT4A-powered 707, was briefly used for the long-range Models 320 and 420 but never quite caught on. *Boeing*

(136,985 kilograms); maximum optional ramp weight 316,000 pounds (143,335 kilograms); maximum typical take-off weight 301,000 pounds (136,531 kilograms); maximum optional take-off weight 316,000 pounds (143,335 kilograms); maximum landing weight 207,500 pounds (94,120 kilograms); maximum zero fuel weight 190,000 pounds (86,183 kilograms); operating weight empty 142,600 pounds (64,682 kilograms); maximum structural payload 47,400 pounds (21,500 kilograms).

**Powerplant:** Four Pratt & Whitney JT4A turbojets. Typical engine model was the JT4A-9 with take-off static thrust of 16,800 pounds (74.7 kN) at sea level on a standard day (59 degrees Fahrenheit/15 degrees Celsius) and maximum continuous static thrust of 13,500 pounds (60 kN). Fuel tank capacity differed according to customer specifications; typical capacity 21,262 U.S. gallons (80,484 liters); maximum optional capacity 23,815 U.S. gallons (90,148 liters).

**Accommodation:** Flight crew of three (captain, first officer, and second officer). Maximum seating for 179 passengers, or 189 passengers if aircraft equipped with four inflatable escape chutes. Typical mixed-class seating for 141 passengers (18 F + 123 Y). Maximum belly cargo volume 1,773 cubic feet (50.2 cubic meters).

**Performance:** Maximum operating speed $V_{mo}$ 339 knots (628 kilometers per hour) at sea level and 378 knots (700 kilometers per hour) at 24,900 feet (7,590 meters) or $M_{mo}$ 0.887 at or above 25,000 feet (7,620 meters); FAR runway length on a standard day + 15 degree Celsius (86 degrees Fahrenheit/30 degrees Celsius) 12,000 feet (3,660 meters); FAR landing runway length on a standard day (59 degrees Fahrenheit/15 degrees Celsius) 7,250 feet (2,210 meters); range with full payload 4,155 nautical miles (7,695 kilometers); range with full mixed-class passengers and bags 5,180 nautical miles (9,595 kilometers); maximum range without payload 5,750 nautical miles (10,650 kilometers).

South African Airways took delivery of the first of its three 707-344s on July 1, 1960. S/N 17928, ZS-CKC, was the 134th 707 built in Renton. *Boeing*

S/N 17608, the last aircraft in the first Pan American order, was delivered on April 28, 1960. After three other owners and numerous leases, this 707-321 was acquired by General Electric in 1986. Re-registered N707GE in June 1990, it then served as a CFM56 testbed based at the Mojave Airport in California where it was photographed on June 7, 1991. *Jim Dunn*

## 707-220

To match the capabilities of the JT4A-powered Douglas DC-8 Series 20 and to meet the need of airlines operating from high-elevation high-temperature airports, Boeing initially planned the 707-220 as a derivative of the JT3C-powered short-body version of the 707-120 with 144-inch fuselage diameter. It progressively evolved with an increase in fuselage width to 148 inches, lengthening of the fuselage to the standard 707-120 long body dimension, addition of 340-U.S. gallon (1,287-liter) wing tip fuel tanks, installation of overwater equipment, and substitution of JT4A-3 engines for the initially intended JT3C-6s. It ended up being ordered only by Braniff Airways with JT4A-3s and standard long-body fuselage but without tip tanks or overwater equipment. Wings and high-lift devices were identical to those of the 707-120.

Only five 707-227s were built, with the first flying on May 11, 1959, certification was obtained six months later in spite of the crash of the first aircraft during an acceptance flight on October 19, 1959. The remaining four -227s were operated by Braniff on its Latin American network until the first quarter of 1971. After service with other operators, the last of the ex-Braniff aircraft was stored in December 1983 and broken up in May 1984.

## Technical Data For the Boeing 707-220

**Dimensions:** Span 130 feet 10 inches (39.88 meters); length overall 145 feet 1 inch (44.22 meters); fuselage length 138 feet 10 inches (42.32 meters); height 42 feet (12.80 meters); fuselage width 12 feet 4 inches (3.76 meters); fuselage height 14 feet 2.5 inches (4.33 meters); wheel base 52 feet 4 inches (15.95 meters); wheel track 22 feet 1 inch (6.73 meters); wing area 2,433 square feet (226 square meters).

**Weights:** Maximum ramp weight 258,000 pounds (117,027 kilograms); maximum take-off weight 257,000 pounds (116,573 kilograms); maximum landing weight 190,000 pounds (86,183 kilograms); maximum zero fuel weight 170,000 pounds (77,111 kilograms); operating weight empty 122,000 pounds (55,338 kilograms); maximum structural payload 40,400 pounds (18,325 kilograms).

**Powerplant:** Four Pratt & Whitney JT4A-3 turbojets with take-off static thrust of 15,800 pounds (70.3 kN) at sea level on a standard day (59 degrees Fahrenheit/15 degrees Celsius) and maximum continuous static thrust of 12,500 pounds (55.6 kN). Fuel tank capacity 17,406 U.S. gallons (65,887 liters).

**Accommodation:** Flight crew of three (captain, first officer, and second officer). Maximum seating for 181 passengers

Optimized for operations from high-elevation/high-temperature airports, five Model 220s were powered by four JT4A-3s but retained the wings and fuse-lage of the long-body Model 120. The first 707-227, S/N 17691, crashed during an acceptance flight on October 19, 1959. The other four went to Braniff International Airways for operations between the United States and South America. *Boeing*

if aircraft equipped with four inflatable escape chutes. Typical mixed-class seating for 142 passengers (28 F + 114 Y). Maximum belly cargo volume 1,668 cubic feet (47.3 cubic meters).

**Performance:** Maximum operating speed $V_{mo}$ 339 knots (628 kilometers per hour) at sea level and 377 knots (698 kilometers per hour) at 24,900 feet (7,590 meters) or $M_{mo}$ 0.88a at or above 24,900 feet (7,590 meters); FAR runway length on a standard day + 15 degrees Celsius (86 degrees Fahrenheit/30 degrees Celsius) 9,600 feet (2,925 meters); FAR landing runway length on a standard day (59° F/15° C) and dry runway 6,700 feet (2,040 meters); range with full payload 2,050 nautical miles (3,795 kilometers); maximum range without payload 4,100 nautical miles (7,595 kilometers).

## 707-420

As soon as the development of its jetliner became known, Boeing was contacted by all major jet engine manufacturers.

Notably, the leading British manufacturer, Rolls-Royce, made it known that its Aero Engine Division had a novel "bypass" turbojet (a.k.a., turbofan) under development. Fitted with a ducted fan ahead of its axial-flow compressor, the Conway turbofan was anticipated to have greater thrust and lower fuel consumption than the JT3C retained for the first 707s. Accordingly, as early as the fall of 1954, Boeing studied variants of its projected 707-8, powered by Rolls-Royce Conway R.Co.5 bypass engines and with take-off weight ranging between 205,000 and 235,000 pounds (92,985 to 106,595 kilograms). The 707-420 intercontinental version, which began with a preliminary layout dated December 30, 1955 for a 296,000-pound (134,263-kilogram) airplane with R.Co.10s, evolved in parallel with the competing Conway-powered DC-8 Series 40.

Identical to the 707-320 in virtually all respects, but powered by Conway turbofans instead of JT4A turbojets, the 707-420 was expected to be particularly attractive to airlines in the British Commonwealth, as these carriers would not have to pay custom duties on British-manufactured engines. However, the first contract for Conway-powered aircraft was not placed by a Commonwealth airline but by Lufthansa, which ordered an initial batch of four 707-430s in April 1956. Although the first Conway-powered had been ordered by the German carrier, the first to fly was one of the 15 707-436s ordered by British Overseas Airways Corporation in October 1956. Ever since that contract was signed, BOAC (which became British Airways in September 1972) has been criticized in the United Kingdom and among anglophiles abroad for ordering Boeing jetliners. However, after the mid-1955 British Government decision to cancel development of the 707-sized Vickers V.1000 military transport from which a VC7 jetliner version was to have been derived, BOAC had been left with a choice of relying on smaller and less economical Comet 4s or ordering American jetliners.

The first Conway-powered 707, an aircraft ordered by BOAC, flew on May 20, 1959 with a temporary U.S. registration. Although the -420 was certificated in the United States on February 12, 1960 under an addendum to the ATC 4A26 for the -320, service entry was delayed until May 1960 by the need to redesign tail surfaces to meet British certification requirements. With the enlarged surfaces, the 707-420 was granted a British certificate by the Air Transport Licensing Board on April 27, 1960.

With the Rolls-Royce bypass turbojet rapidly overtaken by the Pratt & Whitney JT3D turbofan, only 37 Conway-powered aircraft were built, 5 707-430s for Lufthansa, 18 -436s for BOAC and BOAC-Cunard, 6 -437s for Air India, 3 -441s for VARIG, 3 -458s for El Al, and 1 -465 each for Cunard Eagle and BOAC. Nine 707-420s were destroyed in airline service, the first being S/N 17723 of Air India which was damaged beyond economic repair at the Bombay Airport on June 22, 1962. The last to be lost was the U.S.-registered S/N 18411 of Coastal Airways which burnt at the Perpignan Airport in France on October 13, 1983. No Conway-powered -420 aircraft are included by Boeing in its list of active aircraft dated June 30, 1998.

## Technical Data For the Boeing 707-420

**Dimensions:** Span 142 feet 5 inches (43.41 meters); length overall 152 feet 11 inches (46.61 meters); fuselage length 145 feet 6 inches (44.35 meters); height 41 feet 8 inches (12.70 meters); fuselage width 12 feet 4 inches (3.76 meters); fuselage height 14 feet 2.5 inches (4.33 meters); wheel base 59 feet (17.98 meters); wheel track 22 feet 1 inch (6.73 meters); wing area 2,892 square feet (268.7 square meters).

The Brazilian airline VARIG became the largest South American 707 operator (illustrated by its first, S/N 17905, PP-VJA). It supplemented the Conway-powered 707-441s and JT3D-powered -341Bs and -341Cs it ordered from Boeing with numerous pre-owned aircraft. *Boeing*

**Weights:** Maximum ramp and take-off weights 316,000 pounds (143,335 kilograms); maximum landing weight 207,500 pounds (94,120 kilograms); maximum zero fuel weight 190,000 pounds (86,183 kilograms); operating weight empty 142,600 pounds (64,682 kilograms); maximum structural payload 47,400 pounds (21,500 kilograms).

**Powerplant:** Four Rolls-Royce R.Co.12 Conway Mark 508 turbofans with take-off static thrust of 17,500 pounds (77.8 kN) at sea level on a standard day (59 degrees Fahrenheit/15° degrees Celsius) and maximum continuous static thrust of 14,265 pounds (63.5 kN). Fuel tank capacity differed according to customer specifications; typical capacity 21,262 U.S. gallons (80,484 liters); maximum optional capacity 23,815 U.S. gallons (90,148 liters).

**Accommodation:** Flight crew of three (captain, first officer, and second officer). Maximum seating for 179 passengers, or 189 passengers if aircraft equipped with four inflatable escape chutes. Typical mixed-class seating for 141 passengers (18 F + 123 Y). Maximum belly cargo volume 1,773 cubic feet (50.2 cubic meters).

**Performance:** Maximum operating speed $V_{mo}$ 339 knots (628 kilometers per hour) at sea level and 375 knots (695 kilometers per hour) at 23,300 feet (7,100 meters) or $M_{mo}$ 0.852 at or above 23,300 feet (7,100 meters); FAR runway length on a standard day + 15 degrees Celsius (86 degrees Fahrenheit/30 degrees Celsius) 12,000 feet (3,660 meters); FAR landing runway length on a standard day (59 degrees Fahrenheit/15 degrees Celsius) 7,250 feet (2,210 meters); range with full payload 4,225 nautical miles (7,825 kilometers); range with full mixed-class passengers and bags 5,270 nautical miles (9,760 kilometers); maximum range without payload 5,850 nautical miles (10,835 kilometers).

## 720

Whereas the fuselage of the 707-120 had to be enlarged and the -220, -320, and -420 variants developed in response to Douglas' aggressive marketing moves, the Boeing 720 came about as a hastened response to Convair's January 1956 announcement of its Model 22 Skylark (later redesignated Convair 880). Smaller than the JT3C-powered 707-120 and Douglas DC-8 Series 10, the Convair jetliner promised to be faster than its heavier competitors. While Douglas did not succeed with its proposed DC-9, then a smaller four-engined derivative of the DC-8, Boeing responded energetically to the challenge from Convair.

With United Airlines—a carrier which had just selected Series 10 and 20 DC-8s in preference to 707-120s but was known also to need smaller, shorter-ranged jetliners—as its initial target, Boeing started work in earnest on the 707-020 in February 1956. By the first week in March, the Seattle manufacturer had preliminary layouts for no fewer than 12 different configurations.

The baseline 707-020-1 retained the newly adopted 148-inch maximum fuselage

G-ARWD was built for Cunard Eagle Airways but went into service as VR-BBW. After BOAC took over Cunard Eagle in February 1962, this 707-465 reverted to its original registration. Last operated by British Airtours, it was traded back to Boeing in May 1981. *Boeing*

Based in Alaska, Pacific Northern Airlines started jet service between Alaska and Seattle on April 27, 1962 with the first of its two 720-062s (S/Ns 18376 and 18377 respectively registered N720V and N720W) ordered in April 1961. *Boeing*

diameter and 130 foot 10-inch span wings of the 707-120 but had its fuselage shortened from 138 feet 10 inches to 115 feet 6 inches (42.32 to 35.20 meters) and was to be powered by four Rolls-Royce RA-29 Avon turbojets. The -2 had a 1-foot (30.5-centimeter) shorter fuselage and was designed around four Pratt & Whitney JT8A-1 turbojets. The -3, -4, and -9 retained the shorter -2 fuselage but were respectively matched to four Pratt & Whitney JT3C-6, General Electric CJ805, and Rolls-Royce RA-29 turbojets. The -11 and -12 were proposed Avon-powered developments with the -2 fuselage but with reduced gross weight and wings with different aspect and taper ratio.

Proposed with four JT3C-4 turbojets, the -10 had broader wings of reduced span (120 feet/36.58 meters) and area (2,322 square feet/215.7 square meters). The more unusual variants, however, were the twin-engined 707-020-5, -6, and -7 with wings of even more reduced span and area (101 feet 8

inches/30.99 meters and 2,100 square feet/195.1 square meters) and respectively proposed with two RA-29, JT3C-4, and JT4A-1 turbojets.

In spite of frenzied design activities, it appeared for nearly 20 months that Boeing would be unsuccessful in its endeavor to block inroads by Convair into the jetliner market. Initial contracts for the Convair jetliner were announced in June 1956 with TWA, already a 707-120 and -320 customer, and Delta, a DC-8 customer, respectively ordering 30 and 10 880s. By October 1957, TWA had ordered four additional 880s, while the Brazilian carrier REAL had become the first customer for a turbofan-powered derivative of the Convair jetliner (this model eventually was designated the 990). Boeing had yet to receive an order for its 707 derivative.

The new short- to medium-range, reduced capacity descendant of the first Boeing jetliner was first redesignated Model 717, but that proved confusing since military

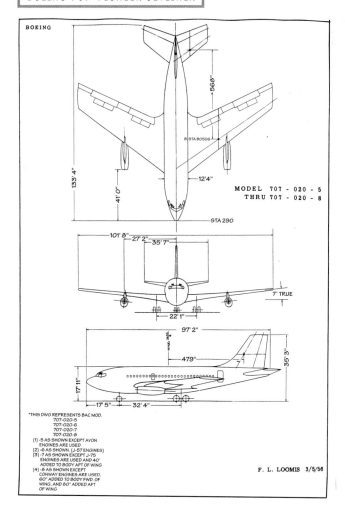

BOEING

568"

B. STA 80.508

133' 4"

12' 4"

41' 0"

MODEL 707 - 020 - 5
THRU 707 - 020 - 8

STA 290

101' 8"
27' 2"
35' 7"

7' TRUE

22' 1"

97' 2"

WING SPAN
479"

35' 3"

17' 11"

17' 5"
32' 4"

*THIS DWG REPRESENTS BAC MOD.
   707-020-5
   707-020-6
   707-020-7
   707-020-8
(1) -5 AS SHOWN EXCEPT AVON
    ENGINES ARE USED
(2) -6 AS SHOWN. (J-57 ENGINES)
(3) -7 AS SHOWN EXCEPT J-75
    ENGINES ARE USED AND 40'
    ADDED TO BODY AFT OF WING
(4) -8 AS SHOWN EXCEPT
    CONWAY ENGINES ARE USED,
    60" ADDED TO BODY FWD. OF
    WING, AND 80" ADDED AFT
    OF WING

F. L. LOOMIS 3/5/56

Before settling on a minimum-change derivative of its 707 to counter the Convair 880, Boeing considered more radical redesigns. This drawing dated May 5, 1956 illustrates a twin-engine 707-020 configuration proposed with either a pair of JT3C, JT4A, or Rolls-Royce Avon turbojets or a pair of Rolls-Royce Conway turbofans. *Boeing*

C/KC-135 variants already used the 717 designation. (Forty years later, that confusion was further compounded when, following the merger with McDonnell Douglas, the Model 717 designation was again used to identify the twinjet MD-95.) Finally, to satisfy the launch customer's wish to have the new aircraft identified by a later numerical designation, it became the Model 720.

With inputs from the airlines, the Model 720 jelled progressively into a more direct derivative of the 707-120. As first sold to United Airlines (UAL) in November 1957, when UAL ordered an initial batch of 11 aircraft, the JT3C-powered Model 720 had a standard 148-inch diameter 707 fuselage with internal cabin length reduced to 96 feet, 6 inches/29.41 meters from the 104-foot, 10-inch/31.95-meter length of the -120 cabin. The shorter cabin of the 720 provided accommodation for 88 first-class passengers, a maximum of 141 economy-class passengers, or 115 passengers in a 30/70 mixed-class arrangement. The basic wing layout of the 707-120 was retained but the wing leading-edge inboard of the inner engines was extended forward to form a "glove," thus increasing the wing chord and reducing the thickness/chord ratio for flights at higher speeds. The never-exceed Mach increased from 0.895 for the 707-120 to 0.906 for the 720-020, while fuel consumption was reduced.

Direct weight reductions resulting from the shorter fuselage and smaller number of seats, galleys, and lavatories also made possible the use of a lighter undercarriage and the deletion of one of the three turbocompressors for the cabin conditioning system. Thus, operating weight empty was reduced nearly eight percent from 118,000 pounds (53,524 kilograms) for the 707-120 to 110,800 pounds (50,258 kilograms) for the 720. Power for the lighter Model 720 was provided by either four Pratt & Whitney JT3C-7s without water injection or four JT3C-12s with water injection, take-off thrust rating being 12,000 pounds (53.4 kN) for the former and 13,000 pounds (58.2 kN) for the latter. Airfield performance was improved due to the lower power and wing loadings but also by the addition of additional Krüger leading-edge flaps outboard of the engines.

Next to contract for 720s was American Airlines (with its order for 25 720-023s later changed to include a mix of turbojet- and turbofan-powered aircraft) bringing the Boeing's order book to a total of 187 jetliners by the time Pan American started 707-121 operations in October 1958. That order book then included 62 707-120s, 5 -220s, 60 -320s, 24 -420s, and 36 Model 720s for a 39-percent share of the four-engine jetliner business. Four competitors, Douglas and Convair in the United States plus Vickers and de Havilland in the United Kingdom, respectively reported orders for 138 DC-8s in four variants, 87 Model 880s and 990s, 35 VC10s, and 33 Comet 4s. Although it led the pack, Boeing was nevertheless in a less than satisfactory position as the production break-even point for its early jetliners had been pushed further into the future by additional costs incurred in developing four additional models to fight off the competition.

The 720 prototype, S/N 17907 intended for United Airlines, first flew from Renton on November 23, 1959. Being sufficiently different from both the 707-100 and 707-300 already FAA-certificated, the 720 was covered by a new Approved Type Certificate, 4A28, issued on June 30, 1960. In the end, Boeing sold only 64 turbojet-powered 720s, one less than recorded by Convair for its commercially unsuccessful Model 880. The seven 720 customers were United Airlines (29 720-022s), American Airlines (10 -023s later re-engined with JT3D turbofans as -023Bs), Eastern Air (15 -025s), Braniff Airways (5 -027s), the Federal Aviation Agency (1 -027), Aer Lingus (3 -048s), and Pacific Northern Airlines (2 -062s).

Two JT3C-powered 720s were lost while operated by other than their original owners (S/N 18423 on September 13, 1974 and S/N 18044 on April 22, 1976). In addition, S/N 18066, previously owned by the FAA, was intentionally crashed at Edwards AFB, California, on December 1, 1984 while radio-controlled to a belly landing short of the runway and into obstacles during a NASA test of a fuel additive designed to lessen hazards associated with burning fuel during an aircraft accident. Although three 720s were still included by Boeing in its June 30, 1998 list of active aircraft, these two Indian-registered and one Zaire-registered aircraft have been stored for the past several years.

## Technical Data For the Boeing 720

**Dimensions:** Span 130 feet 10 inches (39.88 meters); length overall 136 feet 9 inches (41.68 meters); fuselage length 130 feet 6 inches (39.78 meters); height 41 feet 6.5 inches (12.66 meters); fuselage width 12 feet 4 inches (3.76 meters); fuselage height 14 feet 2.5 inches (4.33 meters); wheel base 50 feet 8 inches (15.44 meters); wheel track 21 feet 11 inches (6.68 meters); wing area 2,510 square feet (233.2 square meters).

**Weights:** Maximum typical ramp weight 213,000 pounds (96,615 kilograms); maximum optional ramp weight 230,000 pounds (104,326 kilograms); maximum typical take-off weight 213,000 pounds (96,615 kilograms); maximum optional take-off weight 229,000 pounds (103,873 kilograms); maximum landing weight 175,000 pounds (79,379 kilograms); maximum zero fuel weight 149,000 pounds (67,585 kilograms); operating weight empty 110,800 pounds (50,258 kilograms); maximum structural payload 28,200 pounds (12,791 kilograms).

**Powerplant:** Four Pratt & Whitney JT3C turbojets. Typical engine model was the JT3C-7 with take-off static thrust of 12,000 pounds (53.4 kN) at sea level on a standard day (59 degrees Fahrenheit/15 degrees Celsius) and maximum continuous static thrust of 10,000 pounds (44.5 kN). Fuel tank capacity differed according to customer specifications; typical capacity 11,850 U.S. gallons (44,856 liters); maximum optional capacity 13,560 U.S. gallons (51,329 liters).

**Accommodation:** Flight crew of three (captain, first officer, and second officer). Maximum seating for 141 passengers. Typical mixed-class seating for 131 passengers (30 F + 101 Y). Maximum belly cargo volume 1,380 cubic feet (39.1 cubic meters).

**Performance:** Maximum operating speed $V_{mo}$ 378 knots (700 kilometers per hour) at sea level and 399 knots (739 kilometers per hour) at 23,400 feet (7,130 meters) or $M_{mo}$ 0.906 at or above 23,400 feet (7,130 meters); FAR runway length on a standard day + 15 degrees Celsius (86 degrees Fahrenheit/30 degrees Celsius) 11,000 feet (3,355 meters); FAR landing runway length on a standard day (59 degrees Fahrenheit/15 degrees Celsius) 6,300 feet (1,920 meters); range with full payload 2,120 nautical miles (3,925 kilometers); range with full mixed-class passengers and bags 2,465 nautical miles (4,565 kilometers); maximum range without payload 3,110 nautical miles (5,760 kilometers).

## 720B

Although preceded into the air and in service by the JT3D-powered 707-120B, the 720B is described first as it was the need for a turbofan-powered version of the 720 to match the Convair 990 which brought Pratt & Whitney to develop the JT3D turbofan and Boeing to offer this turbofan not only for a 720 version but also for 707-120 and -320 derivatives.

Having ordered 707-123s in November 1955 when it became the second customer for Boeing jetliners, American Airlines amended its order in July 1958, canceling five JT3C-powered 707-123s but ordering 25 like-engined 720-023s. Notwithstanding its 720 orders, American Airlines remained interested in the slightly smaller 990 which Convair was aggressively marketing with General Electric CJ-805-21 engines with a fan mounted behind the turbine. Fearing that American Airlines would reduce or cancel altogether its 720 order if Convair succeeded in promoting its 990 for luxury high-speed service to complement standard but slower 707-120 service, Boeing felt that it needed to have a turbofan-powered airliner. To achieve this goal, the Seattle manufacturer turned to Pratt & Whitney which, in mid-February 1958, had initiated the self-financed definition phase for a JT3D turbofan derivative of the JT3C turbojet with a two-stage fan and single-stage stator mounted ahead of the axial-flow compressor.

With its engineering staff reacting enthusiastically to the greater power, lower fuel consumption, and reduced noise promised by turbofan engines, American Airlines ordered 25 Convair 990s in October 1958. It also forcefully maneuvered

Boeing into accelerating its development of turbofan-powered versions of its 707 and 720 and offering these derivatives at "bargain basement" prices. After haggling with Boeing for nearly a year, American finally renegotiated its contracts to have its 707-123s and 720-023s either re-engined with JT3Ds or delivered with these turbofans. Availability of JT3D-powered Boeing jetliners effectively ended Convair's hopes to remain an effective participant in the transport aircraft business. Only 37 Convair 990s were built while Boeing went on to build 644 JT3D-powered 707-120s, -320Bs, and -320Cs for airlines, to re-engine 49 707-120s and 720s, and to deliver 126 JT3D-powered derivatives to government and military customers. For Boeing, the development of the 720B to meet American Airlines' demands had proven an expensive undertaking, but it ended up firming up its position as the world's foremost jetliner manufacturer.

The first JT3D-powered 720-023B flew on October 6, 1960, 3 1/2 months after the first JT3D-powered 707-123B. The Approved Type Certificate for the 720, ATC 4A28, was amended on March 3, 1961 to cover the 720B, and Boeing went on to build 89 JT3D-powered 720Bs for 10 airlines: 12 720-023Bs for American Airlines, 3 American-ordered -023Bs for Pan American, 8 -024Bs for Continental Airlines, 8 -030Bs for Lufthansa, 4 -040Bs for Pakistan International Airlines, 27 -047Bs for Western Airlines, 17 -051Bs for Northwest Orient Airlines, 2 -058Bs for El Al, 3 -059Bs for Avianca, 3 -060Bs for Ethiopian Airlines, and 2 -068Bs for Saudia. Boeing also re-engined 10 turbojet-powered 720-023s for American Airlines. The 720B went into service on March 12, 1961, and the last 720B was delivered to Western on September 20, 1967.

No fewer than 20 of the 99 720Bs were destroyed while in airline service. However, this dubious record is not due to defective design, poor maintenance, or substandard flying, as 11 of these aircraft were lost in shelling of the Beirut International Airport by various warring factions. In that respect, it is worth noting that over the years "criminally minded" Palestinian terrorists accounted for the destruction of only two 707s while "peace-loving" Israeli defense forces contributed directly to the loss of at least eight 707s and 720s at the Beirut Airport. Fighting between Palestinian refugees and Christian Lebanese forces accounted for another five Boeing jetliners. Sadly, regardless of their religious allegiances, "valiant" Middle East warriors have not done much to further airline safety and ended covering themselves with shame.

Boeing's list of active aircraft on June 30, 1998 include seven 720Bs, but the only two flown during the previous 12 months, albeit only briefly, were the Pratt & Whitney Canada engine testbed (S/N 18024 ex 720-023B of American Airlines) and the Allied Signal test bird (S/N 18384 ex 720-051B of Northwest Orient Airlines).

## Technical Data For the Boeing 720B

**Dimensions:** Span 130 feet 10 inches (39.88 meters); length overall 136 feet 9 inches (41.68 meters); fuse-

This underside view of a 720-023 for American Airlines shows to advantage the "glove" extension on the inboard section of the wing leading edge. This modification reduced the thickness/chord ratio and enabled the never-exceed Mach number to be increased from 0.895 to 0.906. *Boeing, courtesy of Peter M. Bowers*

lage length 130 feet 6 inches (39.78 meters); height 41 feet 6.5 inches (12.66 meters); fuselage width 12 feet 4 inches (3.76 meters); fuselage height 14 feet 2.5 inches (4.33 meters); wheel base 50 feet 8 inches (15.44 meters); wheel track 21 feet 11 inches (6.68 meters); wing area 2,510 square feet (233.2 square meters).

**Weights:** Maximum typical ramp weight 222,000 pounds (100,698 kilograms); maximum optional ramp weight 235,000 pounds (106,594 kilograms); maximum typical take-off weight 222,000 pounds (100,698 kilograms); maximum optional take-off weight 234,000 pounds (106,141 kilograms); maximum landing weight 175,000 pounds (79,379 kilograms); maximum typical zero fuel weight 147,000 pounds (66,678 kilograms); maximum optional zero fuel weight 156,000 pounds (70,760 kilograms); operating weight empty 115,000 pounds (52,163 kilograms); maximum structural payload 41,000 pounds (18,595 kilograms).

**Powerplant:** Four Pratt & Whitney JT3D turbofans. Typical engine model was the JT3D-1 with take-off static thrust of 17,000 pounds (75.6 kN) at sea level on a standard day (59 degrees Fahrenheit/15 degrees Celsius) and maximum con-tinuous static thrust of 14,500 pounds (64.5 kN). Fuel tank capacity differed according to customer specifications; typical capacity 14,830 U.S. gallons (56,136 liters); maximum optional capacity 16,055 U.S. gallons (60,774 liters).

**Accommodation:** Flight crew of three (captain, first officer, and second officer). Maximum seating for 149 passengers, or 156 passengers if aircraft equipped with four inflatable escape chutes. Typical mixed-class seating for 137 passengers (18 F + 119 Y). Maximum belly cargo volume 1,380 cubic feet (39.1 cubic meters).

**Performance:** Maximum operating speed $V_{mo}$ 378 knots (700 kilometers per hour) at sea level and 399 knots (739 kilometers per hour) at 23,300 feet (7,100 meters) or $M_{mo}$ 0.90 at or above 23,300 feet (7,100 meters); FAR runway length on a standard day + 15 degrees Celsius (86 degrees Fahrenheit/30 degrees Celsius) 7,500 feet (2,285 meters); FAR landing runway length on a standard day (59 degrees Fahrenheit/15 degrees Celsius) 6,600 feet (2,035 meters); range with full payload 2,085 nautical miles (3,860 kilometers); range with full mixed-class passengers and bags 3,300 nautical miles (6,110 kilometers); maximum range without payload 3,910 nautical miles (7,240 kilometers).

The 720 first flew from Renton on November 23, 1959. Intended for United Airlines (hence its N7201U registration), this 720-022 was initially flown in the manufacturer's scheme illustrated by this photo dated December 3, 1959. *Boeing*

This ex-Braniff International Airways 720-027 was later acquired by American Aviation Services. Registered N736T while on lease to Aeroamerica, it is seen here while subleased to Saudi Arabian Airlines during the summer of 1977. *Jelle Sjoerdsma*

## 707-120B

While the 720B was under development, the merit of incorporating the "glove" wing leading-edge extension and turbofan engines into the larger 707-120B became increasingly obvious to Boeing and American Airlines. Other Boeing customers were not long to appreciate the potential offered by these wing and engine upgrades, notably in terms of improved field performance and reduced fuel consumption. Not surprisingly, orders for the resulting 707-120B version rapidly mounted.

The first of these aircraft, a 707-123B for American Airlines, flew on June 22, 1960, and ATC 4A21 was amended on March 1, 1961 to cover the -120B in its "long body" version for most airlines. An additional amendment was approved on July 24, 1961 to cover the "short body" 707-138B version for Qantas. Aircraft covered by these amendments included 78 new-built aircraft (31 -123Bs for American, 41 -131Bs for TWA, and 6 -138Bs for Qantas) as well as 39 Model 120s modified and re-engined for Pan American (5 -121s as -121Bs and 1 -139 as a -139B), American (23 -123s as -123Bs), Qantas (7 -138s as -138Bs), and the USAF (3

-153/VC-137As as -153Bs/VC-137Bs). Deliveries of the originally sized 707 ended on January 23, 1969 when TWA accepted S/N 20057, the last of its 707-131Bs.

Only three 707-120Bs were destroyed in airline service between January 16, 1974 and November 30, 1980, all three being damaged beyond economical repair in ground accidents. Nevertheless, being less economical to operate than more capacious 707-320B/Cs, 707-120Bs did not fare well in their later years. On June 30, 1998, Boeing included only seven -120Bs in its list of active aircraft. None had been flown during the previous 12 months.

## Technical Data For the Boeing 707-120B

**Dimensions:** Span 130 feet 10 inches (39.88 meters); length overall 144 feet 6 inches (44.04 meters); fuselage length 138 feet 10 inches (42.32 meters); height 42 feet (12.80 meters); fuselage width 12 feet 4 inches (3.76 meters); fuselage height 14 feet 2.5 inches (4.33 meters); wheel base 52 feet 4 inches (15.95 meters); wheel track 22 feet 1 inch (6.73 meters); wing area 2,510 square feet (233.2 square meters).

**Weights:** Maximum typical ramp weight 258,000 pounds (117,027 kilograms); maximum typical take-off weight 258,000 pounds (117,027 kilograms); maximum landing weight 190,000 pounds (86,183 kilograms); maximum zero fuel weight 170,000 pounds (77,111 kilograms);

Yet to see sand, the first 720-068B for Saudi Arabian Airlines poses for a Boeing photographer over snow-covered fields prior to its delivery on December 20, 1961. *Boeing*

Ethiopian Airlines ordered a first pair of 720-060Bs in July 1960 but these aircraft, S/Ns 18165 and 18166, which first flew in November 1961, were delivered to Saudi Arabian Airlines. Their place and registrations, ET-AAG and ET-AAH, were given less than one year later to two new 720-060Bs, S/Ns 188453 and 18454. *Boeing*

operating weight empty 127,500 pounds (57,833 kilograms); maximum structural payload 42,500 pounds (19,280 kilograms).

**Powerplant:** Four Pratt & Whitney JT3D turbojets. Typical engine model was the JT3D-1 with take-off static thrust of 17,000 pounds (75.6 kN) and maximum continuous static thrust of 14,500 pounds (64.5 kN). Fuel tank capacity differed according to customer specifications; typical capacity 15,408 U.S. gallons (58,324 liters).

**Accommodation:** Flight crew of three (captain, first officer, and second officer). Maximum seating for 179 passengers, or 189 passengers if aircraft equipped with four inflatable escape chutes. Typical mixed-class seating for 142 passengers (20 F + 122 Y). Maximum belly cargo volume 1,668 cubic feet (47.3 cubic meters).

**Performance:** Never-exceed speed $V_{ne}$ 385 knots (713 kilometers per hour) or $M_{ne}$ 0.895 Mach; maximum operating speed $V_{mo}$ 379 knots (702 kilometers per hour) at sea level and 399 knots (739 kilometers per hour) at 23,000 feet (7,010 meters) or $M_{mo}$ 0.90 at or above 23,000 feet (7,010 meters); FAR runway length on a standard day + 15 degrees Celsius (86 degree Fahrenheit/30 degrees Celsius) 9,400 feet (2,865 meters); FAR landing runway length on a standard day (59 degrees Fahrenheit/15 degrees Celsius) and dry runway 6,500 feet (1,980 meters); range with full payload 2,640 nautical miles (4,890 kilometers); range with full mixed-class passengers and bags 3,545 nautical miles (6,565 kilometers); maximum range without payload 4,325 nautical miles (8,010 kilometers).

## 707-320B

The greater thrust and reduced fuel consumption of the JT3D were possibly of greater value to heavy long-range jetliners. Yet, having pioneered the use of JT3Ds with its 707-120B and 720B, Boeing was outpaced by rival Douglas when it came to using these turbofans to power long-range aircraft. Philippines

Airlines became the first customer for JT3D-powered DC-8 Series 50 when it ordered two in May 1959. Douglas flew the first Series 50 on December 20, 1960 and obtained certification for this Series 30-derivative on May 1, 1961. The first JT3D-powered Boeing 707-320Bs were ordered by Pan American only in February 1961, and this variant first flew on January 31, 1962. The Approved Type Certificate 4A26 was amended by the FAA on May 31, 1962 to cover the Model 320B, and Pan American began 707-321B operations the following day.

In addition to being powered by JT3Ds turbofans instead of JT4A turbojets, Model 320Bs differed from Model 320s in having wings of increased span and area as the result of the addition of extended outboard panels with curved wing tips, leading-edge extended forward between the fuselage and inboard engines, and revised trailing-edge flaps. Late production aircraft, referred to as Advanced 707-320Bs, added two segments of Krüger leading-edge flaps, further modifications of the trailing-edge flaps, and revised fan cowlings with larger blow-in doors to increase airflow on take-off. With all modifications, maximum certificated gross take-off weight was increased to 335,000 pounds (151,953 kilograms).

Four aircraft built for Northwest Orient Airlines with the 707-351B (SCD) model designation were the first 707s since the 367-80 to be fitted with side cargo doors (hence the SCD in their designation). Located forward of the wing on the port side of the fuselage for loading and unloading cargo on the main deck, the upward-hinging SCD measured 91x134 inches (2.31x3.40 meters). Although the 707-351B (SCD)s were ordered as convertible aircraft and could carry freight, passengers, or mixed passenger/cargo loads, they lacked the reinforced flooring of the more fully modified 707-320Cs. The first 707-351B (SCD) flew on May 15, 1963, nearly three months after the first 707-351C for Pan American.

Including the four hybrid -351B (SCD)s for Northwest, Boeing built a total of 170 Model 320Bs for airlines customers with aircraft for late customers being identified by alpha-numeric designations after the manufacturer ran out of two-digit customer numbers. Aircraft built for airlines included 3 707-312Bs for Malaysian Singapore, 60 -321Bs for Pan American, 10 -323Bs for American, 8 -328Bs for Air France, 12 -330Bs for Lufthansa, 2 -336Bs for BOAC, 3 -337Bs for Air India, 2 -344Bs for South African Airways, 6 -351Bs and 4 -351B (SCD)s for Northwest, 3

A LAN-Chile 707-330B, ex-Lufthansa, taxies in the fog for an early morning departure from the Aeropuerto Internacional Jorge Chávez in Lima, Peru, in 1975. The Chilean carrier had begun 707 service from Santiago to New York eight years earlier. *René J. Francillon*

-358Bs for El Al, 2 -359Bs for Avianca, 7 -382Bs for TAP, 2 -384Bs for Olympic, 4 -387Bs for Aerolineas Argentinas, and 4 -3J6Bs for CAAC. In addition, Boeing built 4 aircraft for non-airline customers (2 707-353Bs as presidential VC-137Cs for the USAF, 1 -3F3B for the government of Argentina, and 1 -3L6B for the Malaysian government).

The last passenger-only 707 to be delivered to an airline was S/N 20457, a 707-336B which was handed over to BOAC on April 17, 1971. A number of passenger-configured 707-320Bs were later con-

Four aircraft were built for Northwest with side cargo doors as fitted to convertible and all-freight Model 320Cs. These 707-351B (SCD)s were delivered in 1963 without the reinforced main-deck flooring of the 320Cs. *Boeing*

verted as freighters, while others were fitted with hushkits as described under the 707-320C heading.

Between December 12, 1968, when a Pan American 707-321B crashed into the sea off the Venezuelan coast, and January 31, 1993, when a 707-387B of Argentina's Lineas Aéreas del Estado was damaged beyond repair in a landing accident at Recife, Brazil, 21 Model 320Bs have been destroyed. Seventeen of these aircraft were lost in flying accidents, including a Korean Air 707-321B shot down by Soviet fighters. Four were destroyed in non-flying accidents, including a TWA -331B and a Pan American -321B destroyed on the ground by terrorist bombs. By June 30, 1998, a good many other -320Bs had been withdrawn from use or converted as freighters, leaving 42 Model 320Bs on the Boeing list of active aircraft. Most of those still active have either been fitted with hushkits for service with smaller airlines, mostly in the developing world, or are in service with government and military customers as detailed in a latter chapter.

## Technical Data For the Boeing 707-320B

**Dimensions:** Span 145 feet 8.5 inches (44.41 meters); length overall 152 feet 11 inches (46.61 meters); fuselage length 145 feet 6 inches (44.35 meters); height 42 feet 5 inches (12.93 meters); fuselage width 12 feet 4 inches (3.76 meters); fuselage height 14 feet 2.5 inches (4.33 meters); wheel base 59 feet (17.98 meters); wheel track 22 feet 1 inch (6.73 meters); wing area 2,942 square feet (273.3 square meters).

**Weights:** Maximum typical ramp weight 328,000 pounds (173,272 kilograms); maximum optional ramp weight 336,000 pounds (152,407 kilograms); maximum typical take-off weight 327,000 pounds (148,325 kilograms); maximum optional take-off weight 335,000 pounds (151,953 kilograms); maximum typical landing weight 207,000 pounds (93,894 kilograms); maximum optional landing weight 247,000 pounds (112,037 kilograms); maximum typical zero fuel weight 190,000 pounds (86,183 kilograms); maximum optional zero fuel weight 195,000 pounds (88,450 kilograms); operating weight empty 148,800 pounds (67,132 kilograms); maximum structural payload 46,200 pounds (20,955 kilograms).

**Powerplant:** Four Pratt & Whitney JT3D turbofans. Typical engine model was the JT3D-3 with take-off static thrust of 18,000 pounds (80.1 kN) on a standard day (59 degrees Fahrenheit/15° degrees Celsius) and maximum continuous static thrust of 16,400 pounds (72.9 kN). Fuel tank capacity 23,855 U.S. gallons (90,299 liters).

**Accommodation:** Flight crew of three (captain, first officer, and second officer). Maximum seating for 179 passengers, or 189 passengers if aircraft equipped with four inflatable escape chutes. Typical mixed-class seating for 141 passengers (18 F + 123 Y). Maximum belly cargo volume 1,770 cubic feet (50.2 cubic meters).

**Performance:** Maximum operating speed $V_{mo}$ 375 knots (695 kilometers per hour) at sea level and 394 knots (730 kilometers per hour) at 23,000 feet (7,010 meters) or $M_{mo}$ 0.887 at or above 23,000 feet (7,010 meters); FAR runway length on a standard day + 15 degrees Celsius (86 degrees Fahrenheit/30° degrees Celsius) 11,400 feet (3,475

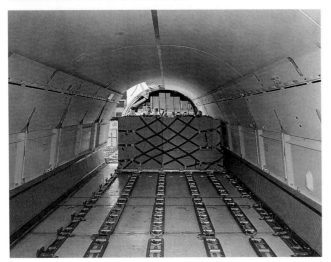

The main deck and side cargo door of the 707-320C made for easy cargo loading at major civil airports. However, the Air Force initially found the similar C-135 installation of limited usefulness, because the need for specialized cargo handling facilities restricted its first jet transports to shuttling between a small number of adequately provided air bases. *Boeing*

meters); FAR landing runway length on a standard day (59 degrees Fahrenheit/15 degrees Celsius) 5,900 feet (1,800 meters); range with full payload 4,275 nautical miles (7,915 kilometers); range with full mixed-class passengers and bags 5,385 nautical miles (9,975 kilometers); maximum range without payload 6,040 nautical miles (11,185 kilometers).

## 707-320C

Combining the basic airframe and powerplant installation of the 707-320B, with all upgrades being similarly introduced during the course of production, with the main deck cargo door of the 707-351B (SCD) and a reinforced cargo floor with tie-downs, the 707-320C was built both as a convertible passenger/cargo aircraft and as a pure freighter. The first 707-321Cs were ordered by Pan American in April 1962, three months after rival DC-8-50CFs had been ordered by Air Canada.

The passenger/cargo convertible 707 first flew on February 19, 1963 and the 707-320C was certificated under an amendment to ATC 4A26 on April 30, 1963. Following the launching of the wide-body 747, most airlines ordered convertible 707-320Cs in preference to all-passenger -320Bs. Production of the convertible aircraft thus greatly surpassed that of earlier passenger variants. In the end, Boeing built 305 Model 320Cs for commercial customers.

Another 707-320C and a -385C were initially retained by Boeing as development aircraft. In addition, Boeing built 29 Model 320Cs for government and military customers as described in another chapter.

Most airlines ordered their -320Cs in convertible passenger/cargo configuration, but a number of customers ordered their aircraft in all-cargo configuration with all passenger amenities (galleys, lavatories, main cabin windows, and emergency oxygen equipment) deleted. This enabled the operating weight empty of all-cargo configured aircraft to be 12,800 pounds (5,810 kilograms) less than that of a convertible aircraft fitted out for passenger operation and 19,600 pounds (8,890 kilograms) less than that of a convertible aircraft fitted out for cargo operation. Payload weight for all-cargo -320Cs was increased in the corresponding proportion.

Converted from the CFM56 test 707-700 aircraft described under the next heading, the last 707-320C was delivered to the Moroccan Government on March 10, 1982, 23 years and seven months after Pan American had taken delivery of the first 707-121.

Not counting the ex-airlines aircraft operated by the USAF and the USN with C-18 and E-8 designations, Boeing included 196 passenger/cargo convertible and all-freight -320Cs in its list of active aircraft as of June 30, 1998. Many of them were operated by air forces and government agencies as detailed in another chapter.

## Technical Data For the Boeing 707-320C

**Dimensions:** Span 145 feet 8.5 inches (44.41 meters); length overall 152 feet 11 inches (46.61 meters); fuselage length 145 feet 6 inches (44.35 meters); height 42 feet 5 inches (12.93 meters); fuselage width 12 feet 4 inches (3.76 meters); fuselage height 14 feet 2.5 inches (4.33 meters); wheel base 59 feet (17.98 meters); wheel track 22 feet 1 inch (6.73 meters); wing area 2,942 square feet (273.3 square meters).

**Weights:** Maximum typical ramp weight 328,000 pounds (173,272 kilograms); maximum optional ramp weight 336,000 pounds (152,407 kilograms); maximum typical take-off weight 327,000 pounds (148,325 kilograms); maximum optional take-off weight 334,000 pounds (151,500 kilograms); maximum landing weight 247,500 pounds (112,265 kilograms); maximum zero fuel weight 220,000 pounds (99,790 kilograms) in passenger configuration or 230,000 pounds (104,326 kilograms) in cargo configuration; operating weight empty 155,100 pounds

| Commercial Customer | Quantity | Model -320C |
|---|---|---|
| Aer Lingus | 4 | -348C |
| Aerolineas Argentinas | 2 | -387C |
| Air France | 8 | -328C |
| | 1 | -355C |
| Air India | 2 | -337C |
| Airlift | 2 | -372C |
| Alia-Royal Jordanian | 2 | -3D3C |
| American | 36 | -323C |
| | 1 | -385C |
| Aviation Services & Support | 1 | -3L6C |
| Braniff | 9 | -327C |
| British Caledonian | 2 | -399C |
| British Eagle | 1 | -365C |
| BOAC | 7 | -336C |
| CAAC | 6 | -3J6C |
| Caledonian | 1 | -365C |
| Camair/Air Cameroun | 1 | -3H7C |
| China Airlines | 2 | -309C |
| Continental | 2 | -321C |
| | 11 | -324C |
| EgyptAir | 9 | -366C |
| El Al | 2 | -358C |
| Ethiopian | 1 | -360C |
| Executive Jet | 2 | -355C |
| Flying Tiger | 4 | -349C |
| Iranair | 4 | -386C |
| Iraqi Airways | 3 | -370C |
| Korean Air | 1 | -3B5C |
| Kuwaiti Airways | 5 | -369C |
| Libyan Arab Airlines | 1 | -3L5C |
| Lufthansa | 6 | -330C |
| MEA | 4 | -3B4C |
| Nigeria Airways | 3 | -3F9C |
| Northwest | 26 | -351C |
| Olympic Airways | 4 | -384C |
| Pakistan International | 7 | -340C |
| Pan American | 34 | -321C |
| Qantas | 21 | -338C |
| Sabena | 7 | -329C |
| Saudia-Saudi Arabian Airlines | 7 | -368C |
| South African Airways | 5 | -344C |
| Sudan Air | 2 | -3J8C |
| Tarom | 4 | -3K1C |
| TWA | 15 | -331C |
| | 2 | -373C |
| VARIG | 3 | -341C |
| | 5 | -345C |
| | 1 | -379C |
| Wardair | 1 | -396C |
| | 1 | -311C |
| Western | 5 | -347C |
| World Airways | 9 | -373C |

(70,352 kilograms) in passenger configuration or 135,500 pounds (61,462 kilograms) in cargo configuration; maximum structural payload 74,900 pounds (33,974 kilograms) in mixed passenger/cargo configuration or 94,500 pounds (42,864 kilograms) in all cargo configuration.

**Powerplant:** Four Pratt & Whitney JT3D turbofans. Typical engine model was the JT3D-3 with take-off static thrust of 18,000 pounds (80.1 kN) on a standard day (59 degrees Fahrenheit/15 degrees Celsius) and maximum continuous static thrust of 16,400 pounds (72.9 kN). Fuel tank capacity 23,855 U.S. gallons (90,299 liters).

**Accommodation:** Flight crew of three (captain, first officer, and second officer). Maximum seating for 195 passengers, or 219 passengers if fitted with automatically deployed and erected escape chutes in compliance with FAR 25.2. Typical mixed-class seating for 141 passengers (18 F + 123 Y). Maximum main deck volume 8,000 cubic feet (226.6 cubic meters) in cargo configuration. Maximum belly cargo volume 1,700 cubic feet (48.2 cubic meters) when aircraft in passenger configuration and 1,785 cubic feet (50.6 cubic meters) in cargo configuration.

**Performance:** Maximum operating speed $V_{mo}$ 375 knots (695 kilometers per hour) at sea level and 394 knots (730 kilometers per hour) at 23,000 feet (7,010 meters) or $M_{mo}$ 0.887 at or above 23,000 feet (7,010 meters); maximum operating altitude, 42,000 feet (12,800 meters); FAR runway length on a standard day + 15 degrees Celsius (86 degrees Fahrenheit/30 degrees Celsius) 11,500 feet (3,505 meters); FAR landing runway length on a standard day (59 degrees Fahrenheit/15 degrees Celsius) 6,300 feet (1,920 meters); range with full payload 2,800 nautical miles (5,185 kilometers); maximum range without payload 6,000 nautical miles (11,110 kilometers).

## Hushkits

In the early seventies, the entry into service of wide-bodied aircraft powered by substantially quieter high-bypass-ratio turbofans rendered operations by noisy first generation jetliners even more conspicuous. Accordingly, Boeing undertook to develop revised JT3D nacelles for its still-in-production 707. These nacelles were tested on a 707-331B (S/N 20059, N8730) leased back from TWA between January and July 1973. However, Boeing did not proceed with this scheme, as airlines showed little interest in noise reduction until the early eighties.

After production of civil 707s ended in 1978, the imposition of new noise emission rules by the FAA (FAR 36 Stage 2) and the International Civil Aviation Organization (ICAO

With plugged cabin windows, this American Airlines 707-323C deserves its Airfreight markings. Owned by George E. Bailey Company since October 1988 and carrying the Liberian registration EL-JNS, this freighter is currently leased by Transway Air International. *Boeing*

Annex 16 chapter 2) suddenly threatened aging but still sprightly 707s (as well as other first-generation jetliners) with enforced early retirement. To enable these aircraft to remain in operation with less wealthy airlines that could not afford new generation jetliners, several companies undertook to develop engine hushkits for JT3D-powered 707s.

The most successful of these hushkit conversions was that developed by Comtran International, Inc. in San Antonio, Texas. Using Rohr Industries' DynaRohr liners and featuring extended intake and fan exhaust ducts, Comtran Q-707 nacelles reduced the 100-EPNdB take-off footprint for a fully loaded 707 from 6.4 to 3.2 miles (10.4 to 5.2 kilometers). Today, most 707s remaining in airline service are fitted with Q-707 nacelle hushkits (for which Comtran sold the rights to Omega Aviation Services in early 1996).

To reduce noise emission still further and bring 707s in compliance with Stage 3 noise requirements, Quiet Skies, Inc. and

Burbank Aeronautical Corporation II were jointly marketing their Stage III hushkit in the late nineties. A 707-3J6B (S/N 20717, N717QS) fitted with these hushkit nacelles was demonstrated at the SBAC Air Show in Farnborough in September 1998.

## 707-700

Powered by four 20,000-pounds (89-kN) class CFM International CFM56 high-bypass-ratio turbofans, the 707-700 was an engine development aircraft using a 707-320C airframe. It first flew on November 27, 1979 and was then presented as the potential prototype for either re-engining existing 707-320B and -320C airframes or for a new production version. However, without a costly fuselage stretch, wing redesign, and strengthened and lengthened undercarriage, the use of CFM56s proved unjustified for new production aircraft. Moreover, re-engining standard airframes was of little interest to major carriers, which by then were standardizing on

This ex-Pan American 707-321C, S/N 19273, was purchased from its third owner by Ecuatoriana in June 1979. It was photographed at the Miami International Airport on February 12, 1982. *R. R. Leader, courtesy of Marty Isham*

Fitted by Boeing with revised JT3D nacelles to reduce noise emission, this 707-331B on lease from TWA makes a low-level fly-by at the Fresno Air Terminal on June 14, 1973 to enable recording to be made during evaluation of the Boeing hushkit. *Boeing*

later generation aircraft, and was too expensive for the smaller airlines building up their fleet with 707-320B/320Cs phased out by their wealthier competitors. Accordingly, plans to re-engine existing aircraft or to build new CFM56-engined 707s were dropped rapidly. Nevertheless, experience gained with the experimental CFM56-engined 707-700 proved valuable for Boeing as this high-bypass-ratio engine was adopted as the standard powerplant for the 737-300 and later variants of the Boeing twinjet and for re-engined KC-135s.

After tests were completed, the experimental -700 was re-engined with JT3Ds and was delivered to the government of Morocco as a 707-3W6C in March 1982. Subsequently, it was modified as a tanker for Al Quwwat al Jawwiya al Malakiya Marakishiya/Force aérienne royale marocaine. As such, it is still in service with this northwest Africa air force.

## Overview

The last direct descendant of the epochal 367-80, an E-3D for the Royal Air Force, first flew on June 14, 1991 bringing to an end the production phase of the first generation of jetliners. There was no doubting that Boeing was the clear winner as that E-3D was the 1,011th aircraft in the series. The series com-

Mostly in the hope of attracting Air Force interest in new tankers or re-engined KC-135s, Boeing built S/N 21956 as a CFM56 test aircraft. Airlines were not interested in this over-powered aircraft, but CFM56s have been adopted to re-engine KC-135A/E/Qs as KC-135R/Ts and RC-135s and to power new-built E-3 export variants and Navy E-6s. *Boeing*

Having failed to anticipate that jet travel would stimulate demand, Convair took a financial bath as its 880 and 990 proved too small and only sold to the tune of 102 aircraft. Even less fortunate, the VC10 (born Vickers but produced by British Aircraft Corporation following the February 1960 reorganization of the U.K. aerospace industry) could have been a formidable challenger but was overly tailored to unrealistic BOAC requirements for its Empire routes and came too late. When the VC10 went into service with BOAC in April 1964, Boeing and Douglas had already obtained firm orders for 380 707/720s and 207 DC-8s. In spite of its passenger appeal, the rear-engined British jetliner was simply too late to attract more than a few customers and only 54 VC10s and Super VC10s were built.

The end of the line for 707 jetliners was in sight when this photograph was taken on June 29, 1973. The aircraft in the foreground is a 707-3J6B for the Civil Aviation Administration of China. President Nixon's unprecedented visit to the People's Republic of China in February 1972 was starting to bear fruits for Boeing! *Boeing*

prised of 1 367-80 demonstrator, 763 Model 707s for airlines and government/military customers, 93 military derivatives (EC-137Ds, E-3s, E-6s and E-8B), and 154 Model 720s.

The runner up, Douglas, which had entered the race from the strength of its undisputed position as the foremost manufacturer of propliners, had bowed out 19 years earlier after delivering its 556th and last DC-8 in May 1972. Third place went to Tupolev which had provided the Soviet response to the Comet and 367-80 with its twinjet Tu-104 derived from the Tu-16 medium bomber. Having achieved a propaganda coup, the Russian manufacturer then was unable to sell its expensive-to-operate and poorly laid-out military/civil hybrid to others than Aeroflot and CSA (Czech Airlines). Including two prototypes of the Tu-110 four-engine derivative, production of the first Soviet jetliner was ended at the 202 mark. De Havilland, which had jump-started the jetliner race, never recovered from the series of Comet 1 accidents and only produced 114 of its beautiful but uneconomical four-engine jetliner.

There also were two "non-starters" in the race for the first jetliner generation. Neither the nearly forgotten Avro Canada C.102 Jetliner, which had first flown on August 10, 1949—just two weeks after the Comet prototype—nor the even less well-known VEB Baade Type 152, which had flown in East Germany on December 4, 1958, got past the flight-test phase.

Success, however, had not come easily for the Seattle manufacturer. Oft-attributed to an alleged Boeing philosophy to offer many different variants of the basic design to meet different airline requirements, the profusion of 707 and 720 models was, as previously detailed, the result of competitive pressures. Unquestionably, Boeing financial officers and its bankers would have preferred to see the company able to limit itself to offering models retaining the wings and fuselage cross-section of the Model 717/KC-135 but providing different seating capacities through changing fuselage lengths. That proved unfeasible when airlines overwhelmingly favored the wider fuselage cross-section of the proposed DC-8. The resulting

| Fuselage Model | Cabin Length | All First-Class Length | All First-Class Seating | All Economy Seating |
|---|---|---|---|---|
| 707-138 & -138B | 128 feet 10 inches 39.27 meters | 94 feet 10 inches | 88 | 147 |
| 720 & 720B | 130 feet 6 inches 39.78 meters | 96 feet 6 inches | 88 | 141 to 156 |
| 707-120, -120B & -220 | 138 feet 10 inches 42.32 meters | 104 feet 10 inches | 96 | 165 |
| 707-320, -320B, -320C & 420 | 145 feet 6 inches 44.35 meters | 111 feet 6 inches | 104 | 179 to 219 |

wider fuselage developed for the 707 was then retained as the company standard until the wide-body 747 was developed. For the 707/720 series, this constant section fuselage was offered in four lengths. However, "slicing the salami" to meet customer requirements was an inexpensive way to offer accommodation ranging from 88 first-class passengers in the short fuselage 707-138 to 219 passengers in the 707-320C in high-density configuration. Even the addition of a reinforced main deck flooring and a main deck cargo door to obtain the 707-320C was relatively inexpensive.

Whereas changes in fuselage length, cabin configuration, and provision for carrying freight on the main deck all proved relatively easy and required limited additional investments, the engineering, manufacturing, and certification for wings of varying span, area, and plan proved expensive for Boeing. Its main competitor, Douglas, had planned its DC-8 with growth in mind and was thus able to keep to a minimum changes to the wings while its jetliner grew from the 265,000-pound (120,202-kilogram) Series 10 to the 355,000-pound (161,025-kilogram) Series 63AF. Conversely, not counting changes in high-lift devices, Boeing ended up having to offer five wing configurations for its first generation of jetliners which grew from the 190,000-pound (86,183-kilogram) 367-80 to the 334,000-pound (151,500-kilogram) 707-320C.

To put it bluntly, Boeing had lacked a sufficient understanding of airline operations when it undertook to develop a jetliner. It was thus forced to react repeatedly to moves by the more savvy Douglas and Convair, which were thoroughly familiar with the needs and preferences of the airlines. To its credit, the Boeing management was willing to make up for errors resulting from this deficient understanding of the air-

line business. While this willingness drastically affected the financial bottom line for several years, it enabled Boeing to acquire the experience on which to build its future supremacy as a jetliner manufacturer. Significantly, Boeing did so by never repeating the costly errors of having to design too many different versions of its aircraft. Notably, 1,832 of its next jetliner, the 727 trijet, were built with only two different cabin lengths and common wings. The 367-80/707/720 lessons had been well learnt.

## Proposed 707 Models

Then more familiar with the U.S. military contractual practices, which often saw manufacturers' initiatives in proposing new models rewarded with "cost-plus-fee" production contracts, Boeing also came up with a bewildering number of proposed 707 derivatives. As most of these proposals entailed major redesign, it was fortunate for the financial health of the company that none found customers as, having to be commercially priced as opposed to sold on "cost-plus-fee" as were military derivatives, their success would have created a serious fiscal drain.

Often ignored by historians, some of these proposals provide interesting hindsight on the development of the first generation of jetliners and are thus worthy of being illustrated and briefly described. They are listed in chronological order to show trends evolving between the mid-fifties and the early seventies.

Proposed shortly after the Conway-powered intercontinental 707-420 matured, the 707-520 designation first appeared in a preliminary layout dated March 9, 1956. It then called for a 707-120 development with 248,000-pounds (112,490-kilograms) gross weight and Rolls-Royce Conway R.Co.10 engines. This proposal died an early death as U.S.

The 707-138s and -138Bs were the shortest models in the 707/720 family. Named *City of Geelong* after a town in Victoria, southwest of Melbourne, VH-EBL was delivered to Qantas on August 19, 1964 but was withdrawn from use by the Australian carrier after only just over four years in service. *Boeing*

| Models | Span | Wing area |
| --- | --- | --- |
| 360-80 | 130 feet (39.62 meters) | 2,400 square feet (222.9 square meters) |
| 707-120, -138 & -220 | 130 feet 10 inches (39.88 meters) | 2,433 square feet (226 square meters) |
| 707-120B, -138B, 720 & 720B | 130 feet 10 inches (39.88 meters) | 2,510 square feet (233.2 square meters) |
| 707-320 & -420 | 142 feet 5 inches (43.41 meters) | 2,892 square feet (268.7 square meters) |
| 707-320B & -320C | 145 feet 8.5 inches (44.41 meters) | 2,942 square feet (273.3 square meters |

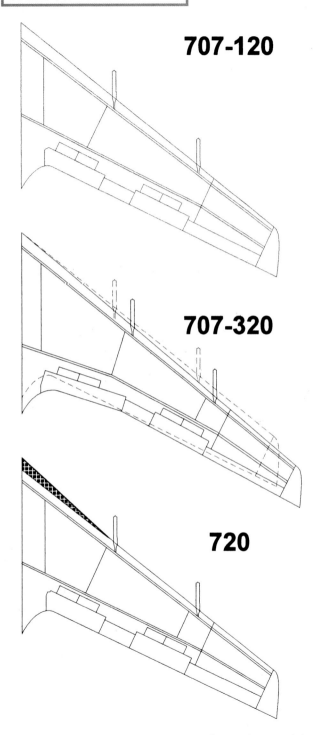

**707-120**

**707-320**

**720**

This drawing shows a comparative plan view of the right wing of the 707-120, 707-320, and 720. *Mark Meredith*

carriers were not interested in a "domestic" aircraft powered by British engines, while airlines in the Commonwealth found the Conway-powered 707-420 more attractive for intercontinental operations. Equally unsuccessful, a later 707-520B layout was prepared for a 707-320B derivative with a 12-foot (3.66-meter) longer fuselage and four 21,000 pounds (93.4 kN) Pratt & Whitney JT3D-5A turbofans.

In the spring of 1956, Boeing studied two configurations to be powered by four proposed Bristol "511" engines. Neither the 248,000-pound (112,490-kilogram) 707-620 based on the 707-120 with a 10-foot (3.05-meter) fuselage extension nor the 296,000-pound (134,265-kilogram) 707-720 derived from the 707-320 got the nod from airlines as the 511 remained a "paper" engine.

Illustrated by a preliminary layout dated April 8, 1957, the 707-320-101 was a proposed 707-320 development with an enlarged lower lobe for additional passenger seating forward of the wing and cargo aft of the main gear well. Reflecting the belief still held by Boeing engineers that jetliners would be used for premium service while "steerage" passengers would be flown in obsolete propliners, this double-deck aircraft was laid-out to accommodate up to 199 first-class passengers, with 159 in the five-abreast upper deck and 40 in the four-abreast lower deck. An alternate cabin configuration provided for 200 coach-class passengers in six-abreast seating on the upper deck and 50 coach passengers in five-abreast seating on the lower deck. With all first-class accommodation in just-introduced, top-of-the-line Lockheed 1649A Starliners providing for only 62 seats in a four-abreast arrangement while all-economy Douglas DC-6Bs sat 102 passengers five abreast, airlines reacted negatively to the overly capacious double-deck Boeing jetliner proposal.

At the beginning of 1960, with the 707-120 and 707-320 well established in revenue service and the Conway-powered 707-420 and lighter 720 about to enter service, Boeing set its sight on developing larger 707 derivatives to achieve lower seat-mile costs. Thus, the 707-520-X was to be a double deck aircraft with low-mounted wings and a fuselage length of 191 feet 7 inches (58.39 meters), while the 707-520-2X was to be similarly configured but with a shorter fuselage. Proposed at the same time, the 707-520-X3 was to be a double deck aircraft with high-mounted wings spanning 142 feet 5 inches (43.41 meters), the same as the 707-320 and -420, but with fuselage length of 144 feet 2 inches (43.94 meters). Airlines judged these proposals to offer excessive capacity while the lack of suitable engines rendered further development of only academic value.

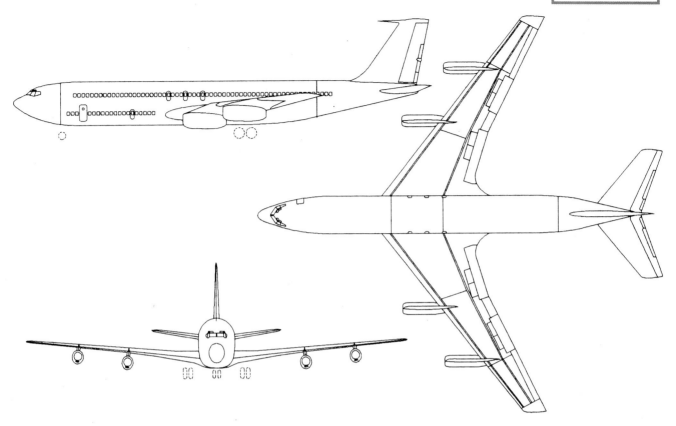

The 707-320-101 was the first large-capacity derivative proposed by Boeing. With accommodation for up to 199 first-class passengers or 250 economy-class passengers, this April 1957 proposal was much too large to attract serious interest from airlines. *Mark Meredith*

When in late 1964 Douglas announced its intent to develop stretched versions of the DC-8 with all-economy seating for up to 259 passengers, Boeing was caught flat-footed. Early on, Boeing had derived much ill-placed pride from the fact that its 707 had a shorter and lighter landing gear than the rival DC-8 and that its first jetliner had a more convenient level fuselage attitude while on the ground whereas the DC-8 had an unsightly Pentatomidae "stinkbug" tail-high attitude on the ground. Later Boeing realized that Douglas, long a proponent of stretching basic designs to increase seating, had wisely chosen a longer gear and tail-up attitude to endow its DC-8 with much growth potential. Unable to match the DC-8-61/63 capacity without an expensive redesign of the main landing gear and inner wing section of its 707, Boeing conceded this segment of the market to Douglas while concentrating its activities on developing a supersonic transport aircraft (the aborted American SST) and the large capacity

747 (then primarily seen as a freighter but also capable of being a "PI" (Passenger Insurance) jetliner in the event that the supersonic transport would fail to materialize in a timely fashion—which it did).

By the early seventies, just as the large-capacity 747 entered service and funding for the supersonic 2707-300 was terminated by Congress, U.S. airlines experienced their worst downturn since the 1930s. As airlines sought to recover by providing more direct point-to-point services and increasing frequencies, Boeing again realized that an aircraft smaller than the 747 and more similarly sized to the stretched DC-8 might be needed. However, it was too late to develop such a derivative and no further 707 developments were undertaken. The last of the first generation jetliners to be delivered to an air carrier, a 707-3F9C, was handed over to Nigeria Airways on January 30, 1978, almost two decades after Pan American had accepted the first 707-121.

One of the last civil 707 built was this Model 370C delivered to Iraqi Airways on August 27, 1974. It got stuck in Amman, Jordan, at the start of the Gulf War in January 1991 and was impounded. *Boeing*

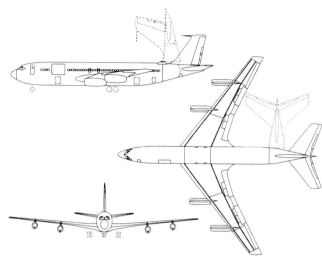

Military-cargo variants of the C-135 and 707 were proposed by Boeing as the Model 735 and Model 738 respectively. Sideways- and upward-swinging tail versions are illustrated. *Mark Meredith*

## Swing-Tail Proposals

Not previously mentioned are freighter 707 derivatives with swing tails. In 1958, when the United States Air Force became painfully aware that its Military Air Transport Service (MATS) was without jet transports, Boeing actively promoted 707 derivatives suitable not only to military operations but also well tailored to commercial air freight operations.

The 367-80 had been designed with side cargo doors, but Boeing was initially unable to attract MATS interest in a transport version of the KC-135. (Ordered under contract AF 33(600)-40063, the first 10 C-135As were funded in the 1960 fiscal year budget.) To spark Air Force interest in a KC-135/707 military transport derivative while offering to airlines a 707 version better suited to air cargo operations, Boeing studied a number of Model 707 and Model 717 derivatives fitted with the tail either swinging sideways or tilting upward to provide unfettered access to the main deck. In a memorandum dated June 25, 1958, Boeing redesignated the 707 commercial cargo derivatives as Model 735s, while military cargo derivatives of either the Model 707 or Model 717 became Model 738s. Representative sideways-swinging tail and upward-tilting tail versions are illustrated. Neither got the nod from military or civil customers, and Models 735 and 738 remained stillborn.

# CHAPTER THREE

# AIRLINE OPERATIONS

The United States entered the jet transport era shortly after 7:00 P.M. on Sunday, October 26, 1958, when a Pan American 707-121 lifted off runway 31L at Idlewild, the New York International Airport. With a cockpit crew of four and seven stewards and stewardesses under the command of 41-year-old Captain Samuel Hudson Miller, a native of Carlisle, Indiana, the pioneering Boeing jetliner was bound for Le Bourget Airport in Paris. Limited to a take-off weight of 212,000 pounds (96,162 kilograms) by noise restrictions imposed by the Port of New York Authority, the aircraft carried a full load of 40 first-class and 71 economy-class passengers

(111 seats being provided in the original Pan American cabin arrangement for the 707-121, then certificated to carry a maximum of 165 passengers in an all-economy layout) and limited mail and cargo.

With this payload, take-off weight restrictions reduced fuel load to 62,500 pounds/28,350 kilograms, about 9,615 U.S. gallons/36,395 liters, not enough for a nonstop flight to Paris. Accordingly, an intermediate fueling stop was required at Gander, Newfoundland, after which the aircraft proceeded "across the pond" to France where it landed 8 hours 55 minutes after leaving Idlewild. Ground time at Gander had been 1 hour 7 minutes, costing $1,500 to Pan American ($8,450 in 1998 dollars) for the landing fee in Newfoundland and additional fuel burned in descent from and climb back to cruising altitude. The aircraft returned from Paris the next day, stopping in Keflavik, Iceland, for 1 hour and 55 minutes to refuel and reaching New York 10 hours 23 minutes after leaving the French capital. Round-trip fares on the inaugural flight were $909 in first class and $489.60 in economy (the equivalent of $5,120 and $2,760 in 1998 dollars, considerably more than what airlines charge in the late 1990s!).

## Initial North Atlantic Operations

Scheduled jet flights across the North Atlantic had been initiated 22 days earlier when, on October 4, 1958, a pair of de Havilland Comet 4s had inaugurated simultaneous BOAC jet service from London to New York and from New York to London. The one-stop westbound flight had taken 10 hours 22 minutes while the nonstop eastbound flight, which benefited from unusually favorable tail winds, only took 6 hours 11 minutes. However, the intended daily BOAC service between London and New York was delayed by labor troubles and the need for the British flag carrier to reschedule its crew-training program.

Pan American also had to contend with labor troubles and daily 707 service was made possible only through the use of supervisory pilots while the carrier and its pilot union negotiated a long-term agreement for jet operations. Moreover, 707-121 operations were plagued by take-off weight restrictions resulting from the Port of New York Authority requirement that jets be at an altitude of not less than 1,200 feet (365 meters) before flying over any community. Overflight of populated areas was indeed a problem for the JT3C-powered 707s, as the use of 1,860 to 2,800 pounds (845 to 1,270 kilograms) of water to increase take-off thrust greatly increased noise and smoke pollution. Consequently, as use of the 9,500-foot (2,895-meter) runway 13R-31L, the longest then available, resulted in overflying either the Rockaway or Howard Beach areas respectively 3.8 and 2.8 miles (6.1 and 4.5 kilometers) from runway ends, the Authority favored the use of runway 25. Wind permitting, take-off from this runway enabled jets to climb over Jamaica Bay. However, as runway 25 was only 8,200-feet (2,500-meters) long, its preferential use imposed reductions in take-off weight.

After initial crew training and prior to commencing scheduled passenger service to Europe, Pan American had briefly utilized its early 707-121s to build up experience by providing cargo service between New York and San Juan, Puerto Rico, and by flying proving and press flights across the North Atlantic. On the eve of the start of scheduled

S/N 17587 was the second 707 built in Renton but was the first to be painted in the Pan American livery. Accordingly, the airline obtained that it be registered out of sequence as N707PA whereas the first aircraft was registered N708PA. Named *Clipper America*, this aircraft was delivered to Pan American on December 19, 1958. *Boeing*

When they could get cabin attendants to move their purses and hats from the sofas, Pan American first-class passengers could enjoy a small lounge located on the left side of the cabin, immediately after the forward entrance door. *Boeing*

operations, one of these press flights benefited from favorable wind conditions and, able to use the longer runway 13R at Idlewild, lifted an adequate fuel load in addition to 115 crew members and non-paying guests to fly nonstop to London. Most early scheduled flights, however, required fueling stops eastbound and especially westbound due to headwind.

During the first two weeks of 707 operations, between October 26 and November 8, 1958, Pan American flew daily between New York and the French capital carrying 540 first-class and 881 economy-class passengers eastbound and 558 first and 972 economy passengers westbound for a better than 95-percent average load factor. Only one of the eastbound flights, that on November 4, was nonstop, flight time and block time for the 707-121 being 7 hours 1 minute and 7 hours 26 minutes. After a dispute with the Italian government, which wanted to impose a surcharge for jet operations, was temporarily settled while the International Air Transport Association worked out an agreement with its members, Pan American extended its Paris service to Rome beginning on November 9, 1958. Pan American next initiated 707-121 service to London on November 16 and to various Caribbean points on December 10, 1959.

## *Clipper Washington* under a Lucky Star

Three months after Pan American had started jet service, business was booming and the airline had already increased accommodation in its 707-121s beyond the original 111-seat, two-class arrangement. However, the airline still faced difficulties as it had not yet resolved its dispute with members of the Air Line Pilots Association (ALPA). Thus, when on February 3, 1959, *Clipper Washington* took off on the second leg of the daily Paris–London–New York flight, its two pilots were from management. Captain W. Waldo Lynch, who had logged 11,185 hours including 350 hours in 707s, was assistant vice president of communications for the airline. The co-pilot was Captain Samuel T. Peters, then chief pilot of Pan Am's Pacific Division, who had logged 14,952 hours including 269 hours in 707s. These two veterans were assisted in the cockpit by J. Laird, navigator, and G. Sinski, engineer. In the two-class cabin two pursers and four stewardesses attended to the needs and comforts of 119 passengers, including the noted actor/dancer/choreographer Gene Kelly.

Bound for New York, with an intermediate fueling stop in Gander, flight PA 115 had taken off from London-Heathrow at 6:45 PM GMT. Two hours later, the plane was cruising at 31,000 feet when Captain Lynch requested and obtained authorization from Oceanic Control to climb to 35,000 feet before entering a frontal system with thunderstorms. As fate would have it, those additional 4,000 feet probably saved the lives of passengers and crew, changing the course of history for the 707 and Boeing.

After the aircraft reached flight level 35 while cruising at Mach 0.82, Captain Lynch left the cockpit to talk with Norman T. Blake, the vice president of Pan Am's Atlantic Division, who was on board as a passenger/observer. Three hours and 20 minutes after take-off, the aircraft was at 52.5 degrees N and 40.5 degrees W, some 500 miles east of Gander. Still in the cabin, Captain Lynch noticed a trim change, accompanied with buffeting and followed by a rapid build-up of acceleration forces. In the cockpit, Captain Peters, who was checking notes on his clipboard after turning left 20 degrees to get on the new course requested by the navigator, also felt buffeting and positive acceleration forces building-up rapidly. Buffeting increased, lights on the co-pilot panel went out, and *Clipper Washington* went into a nosedown spiral to the right. PA 115 was in serious trouble.

While Captain Peters struggled to regain control by applying left aileron and rudder to stop the roll, Captain Lynch had a difficult time negotiating his way back up to the cockpit due to the g-forces. Once back in the cockpit, the first thing he did before even trying to get back into his seat was to pull all the throttles back to idle.

When Capt. Lynch finally got into the left seat he saw the altimeter unwinding fast as the aircraft was passing through 17,000 feet after already losing 18,000 feet of altitude. He could not see the Mach meter, which was hidden by the control wheel. The artificial horizon was useless as it was "caged" and the turn-and-bank indicator was full to the right with its ball left of center. The horizontal stabilizer was in the full nosedown position and the electric trim button refused to work.

Taking over the control, Captain Lynch was assisted by the navigator, who kept calling the altitudes, and the engineer,

Photographed at the Tocumen International Airport during the summer of 1975, but not on the occasion of the story related in the accompanying box, this 707-321B (S/N 19377, N434PA, *Clipper Morning Glory*) was with Pan American between January 1968 and November 1975. On lease to Sudan Airways after it had been acquired by Comtran International Inc., it crashed on approach to Nairobi, Kenya, on December 4, 1990. *René J. Francillon*

who deactivated the stabilizer system and rolled up the two stabilizer wheels to the "up" position. First succeeding in getting the wings level, Lynch pulled back on the yoke as the aircraft passed through 8,000 feet, still going down. Finally, at 6,000 feet there were a few seconds of violent buffeting, but descent stopped and *Clipper Washington* got into a fairly steep climb. At 9,000 feet the crew realized they had things back under control and the rate of climb was reduced. Flying the aircraft manually, Captain Lynch and his crew leveled out at 31,000 feet and cruised to Gander at Mach 0.79. The landing at Gander was uneventful.

Although knocked around, passengers and crew members suffered no serious injuries. The aircraft, however, had suffered what the Civil Aeronautics Board (CAB) described as "extensive structural damage." This included: (1) wrinkles in the lower skin of both horizontal stabilizer with buckles in the center section web and upper surface doubler; (2) damage to both wing panels, including shear wrinkles in the rear spar webs; (3) damage to outboard ailerons and their control rods; (4) damage to the wing-to-fuselage fairings, with a 3-foot section of the right fairing having separated in flight; (5) small amount of permanent set to both wing panels; (6) buckling to all four engine nacelle strut-to-wing fairings; and (7) partial failure of the shear bolts in No. 2 and No. 3 nacelles and elongated fitting holes of all front spar-to-wing bushings.

The CAB concluded its investigation by ascertaining that probable causes were: (1) inattention of the co-pilot in the absence of the captain; (2) the self-disengagement of the autopilot; (3) autopilot disengagement light left in the "dim" position and therefore not easily seen; and (4) Mach trim switch not turned on. Although not cited as a contributory factor, pilot fatigue most likely played a significant role. As it was, management pilots had excessively long duty hours and insufficient rest time as Pan American struggled to maintain a full schedule while its ALPA pilots refused to fly 707s pending resolution of their pay dispute.

One cannot help but wonder what would have happened if Captain Lynch and his crew had not succeeded in regaining control. The loss of *Clipper Washington* in the Atlantic would likely have become an American counterpart to the comet disaster off Elba in January 1954. At best, the 707 would have had to be withdrawn from use pending result of an accident investigation, a process that would have been made lengthy by the difficulty of recovering wreckage from mid-North Atlantic waters. Fortunately for Boeing and the history of jet transport, all is well that ends well.

After the near catastrophe on February 3, 1959, *Clipper Washington* was ferried from Gander to Seattle for thorough inspection by Boeing. Once repairs had been made by the manufacturer, the aircraft (N712PA, S/N 17591) was returned to service. Re-engined with JT3D-1s in 1965, it remained in service with Pan American until February 1974, 15 years after its close call. Leased and then bought by Pan Ayer, it was successively registered in Turkey (as TC-JBD) and Panama (as HP-756, HP-793, and HP-794). Withdrawn from use at Taipei, Taiwan, in 1978, the once lucky aircraft was broken up there in August 1984.

With the availability of its longer-ranged 707-321s, which Pan American placed into service on August 26, 1959 over the "Blue Ribbon" North Atlantic network and used to provide round-the-world jet service beginning on October 18, 1959, the 707-121s were transferred to Caribbean and South American operations where sectors were shorter. Nevertheless, after losing N709PA in a crash near Elkton, Maryland, on December 8, 1963, the "Blue Meatball" carrier had its remaining five -131s re-engined with JT3D turbofans to increase their payload/range. One of the re-engined 707-121Bs was lost in a September 17, 1965 crash in Antigua, and the last four went to THY Turkish Airlines, via Pan Ayers, in February 1975.

Already having gained the distinction of being the first to operate JT3C-powered 707-120s and JT4A-powered -320s, Pan American continued to live up to its "world's most experienced" motto by starting JT3D-powered intercontinental service with the 707-321B on June 1, 1962 and with the convertible 707-321C on June 3, 1963. Altogether, and including aircraft initially ordered and/or delivered to other carriers, Pan American went on to operate 137 Model 707s and 720s. Six were 707-121s (5 converted as -121Bs), 2 ex-Western -139Bs, 20 -321s, 6 -331s diverted from a TWA contract, 60 -321Bs, 34 -321Cs, and 9 ex-American Airlines 720B-023Bs or Lufthansa 720B-030Bs.

Even though Pan American initiated jumbo jet service in January 1970, 11 years and 3 months after its first 707 service, it retained 707s for another 10 years. First to go were the 707-331s, with the last of these TWA-ordered aircraft being retired in November 1973. Over the next 15 months, Pan American phased out its last 707-121Bs, -321s, -139Bs, and 720Bs. Final operations for the 707-321Bs and -321Cs occurred in 1980. In 22 years of worldwide operations, Pan American had lost 12 of its 137 Boeing 707s and 720s (4 in the U.S., 1 in Europe, 1 in the Caribbean, 1 in South America, and 5 in the Asia/Pacific region).

## Overbooking in Pre-Political Correctness Days

Having originated in Buenos Aires and made several intermediate stops on its milk run back to the United States, a Pan American 707 arrived nearly full at Panama's Aeropuerto Internacional de Tocumen. Most passengers were continuing on to Miami and New York, but a few deplaned, while many more expected to board for the next legs to the States. Surprise, surprise, the flight was overbooked! Used to this not infrequent situation at their station, the Pan Am staff at Tocumen went through the usual routine of offering free booking, hotel accommodation, and meals to those passengers prepared to await later flights. There were no volunteers. Time for the next step in the

This 720-023B was delivered to American Airlines in July 1961. Between 1963 and 1972, it flew as N782PA with Pan American. It was leased by Ecuatoriana in January 1975. Registered HC-AZQ and named *Imbabura*, it received this colorful livery designed by an Ecuadorian artist. *René J. Francillon*

prescribed overbooking procedure: offering monetary compensation in addition to later booking, room, and board. Still no takers. The Tocumen staff was at a loss when the seasoned Pan Am captain entered the fray.

Apparently undisturbed by the overbooking situation, he ordered boarding to commence while, with the help of his copilot and flight engineer, he went through the standard cockpit checklist. Midway through the boarding, the shrewd captain announced that there was a minor technical difficulty and that, regrettably, passengers were to return to the boarding lounge while an engineering solution was devised. Complimentary drinks were to help passengers take the delay in stride.

Having noticed earlier that among the passengers there was a group of young men on home leave after working in Venezuelan oil fields, the cunning captain surreptitiously passed his instructions to his senior stew. (In the early years of jetliner operations the politically correct "cabin attendants" had yet to replace "stews" when referring to stewardesses and stewards.) The younger and more attractive stews were to devote particular attention to the young oilmen and to make sure that these unsuspecting "machos" would have unimpeded access to the free bar.

In the next hour, the "technical problem" was fixed and boarding was resumed. This time the devious captain let his copilot and flight engineer handle the checklist procedure so that he could stand at the gate next to the boarding agents. When the unsuspecting young men, feeling good because alcohol made them believe that they had "scored" with the attractive stewardesses, arrived at the gate, the captain was ready for them. Dutifully invoking the almighty FARs (Federal Aviation Regulations), he ordered the inebriated young men be denied boarding. Miraculously, there were enough seats for all the other passengers and the flight departed without further delay. Problems were easier to solve in the days before political correctness was invented!

## With U.S. Carriers

With U.S. domestic airlines, the Boeing jetliner was introduced into service not by a 707 customer but by a DC-8 customer. Wanting to beat Eastern Air, its arch rival on the lucrative New York–Miami route, National Airlines negotiated a 707-121 dry-lease agreement with Pan American pending availability of the DC-8s, which it had been the first to order (not finalized until later, the National order had come close to fruition even before Pan American concluded its October 1955 order for 707-121s and DC-8-31s) and invested in training pilots for short-duration 707 operations. Training was completed in time for 707 service to begin on December 10, 1958, enabling National to capture the lion's share of that year-end holiday traffic.

Sustained 707 operations within the continental United States were inaugurated by American Airlines on January 25, 1959 when it placed the 707-123 in service on the prestigious New York–Los Angeles transcontinental route, beating rivals TWA (which began 707-131 service on March 20, 1959) and United (which started DC-8-10 operations on September 18, 1959). Tragically, American became the first airline to lose a U.S.-built airliner as its 14th 707-123 crashed on approach to the Grumman airfield in Calverton, New York, during a training flight on August 15, 1959, killing five American Airlines instructors and trainees. The New York-based carrier (it moved its headquarters to Dallas in 1979) had better luck in 1961, when it made further marks on early jetliner history by introducing turbofan-powered aircraft into service, the 720-023B on March 12 and the 707-123B less than three months later.

American Airlines went on to operate a total of 128 707/720s, including 25 707-123s (all but two re-engined with JT3Ds as -123Bs), 31 -123Bs, 10 -323Bs, 36 -323Cs, 1 -385C, and 25 720-023/023Bs (the first 10 being delivered as JT3C-powered -023s and later upgraded as turbofan-powered -023Bs, while the last 15 were JT3D-powered on delivery). The 720Bs were withdrawn from use in 1971, after only 10 years in service with the carrier which had pushed for its development, but American Airlines retained 707s for another 12 years, its last 707-323B/Cs being sold in 1983.

Caught in an imbroglio for corporate control between Howard Hughes and other shareholders, TWA lost valuable time in getting into the jet age as Hughes favored the smaller but faster Convair 880. While awaiting its 880s, which it was able to place into service only in January 1961, TWA began 707-131 domestic service on March 20, 1959 and transatlantic service to London with the 707-331 on November 23, 1959. Its fleet of 707s eventually grew to 125 aircraft, including 15 -131s, 3 ex-Continental -124s, 41 -131Bs, 12 -331s, 37 -331Bs, 15 -331Cs, and 2 -373Cs initially ordered by World Airways. It also leased two 720-051Bs in 1961–1962.

Among other U.S. carriers which flew first generation Boeing jetliners, Northwest Orient Airlines deserves to be singled out. This Minneapolis-based carrier had become a relatively late entrant in the jetliner race when ordering five DC-8 Series 30s in June 1958. In March 1961, 10 months after receiving its first DC-8, NWA had ordered six Boeing 720Bs. Dissatisfied with the performance shortfall of its early DC-8-30s and finding Boeing product support to be more effective than that provided by Douglas, Northwest accepted in May 1962 a Boeing offer to dispose of its DC-8s in partial trade for the start of a new fleet of 707-351Bs, including four aircraft fitted with a main deck cargo door. Northwest never looked back to Douglas for four-engine jetliners and went on to acquire 53 of the first generation Boeing jetliners (10 Model -351Bs, 26 -351Cs, and 17 model 720-051Bs). Effectively, this marked the beginning of the end for Douglas. After ostentatiously failing to listen to and react appropriately to complaints from Northwest and other long-time customers, the Southern California firm never regained the lead. Thirty-five years later, after its successive Santa Monica, Long Beach, and St. Louis lords and masters often ignored the needs of airline customers, it ignominiously ended up being absorbed into the Seattle-based master jetliner builder.

Better known as DC-8 customers, United Airlines and Eastern Air Lines were instrumental in getting Boeing to develop the

N18712, a 707-331B of TWA, on final approach with flaps and gear down. After being bought back by Boeing in April 1984, this aircraft contributed its engines and horizontal tail surfaces to the KC-135E program. *Bill Curry, courtesy Marty Isham*

reduced capacity Model 720 for domestic operations. Eventually acquiring a total of 29 JT3C-7 powered 720-022s, United became the first to operate this model when it placed it into service on July 5, 1960 on the Chicago–Denver–Los Angeles route where the lighter power loading of the 720 proved particularly beneficial to cope with the higher elevation and higher ambient summer temperatures of the Colorado airport. United finally stored its last 720s in 1973. Eastern Air Lines, which had only acquired 15 Model 720-025s, traded these aircraft back to Boeing in 1970 to build up its 727-225 fleet.

Equally noteworthy was Braniff, which ordered five of the unique 707-227s. Retaining the long-body airframe of the 707-120, these aircraft were powered by JT4As in order to have added thrust for operations from high elevation/high ambient temperature airports on its South American network (La Paz, Bolivia, 13,355 feet/4,070 meters above ground level (AGL); Quito, Ecuador, 9,226 feet/2,812 meters; and Bogota, Colombia, 8,355 feet/2,547 meters). The first of these aircraft was lost in a pre-delivery acceptance flight on October 19, 1959 when training pilots got carried away while attempting violent "out-of-the-envelope" maneuvers at low speed. Three engines were torn off at 12,000 feet (3,660 meters) and the Boeing training captain was unsuccessful in his attempt to crash land the aircraft on the power

of the single remaining engine. The aircraft struck a small island near Arlington, WA, and four pilots, including the Boeing instructor, were killed. Four others, who were seating aft in the main cabin, survived the crash. Braniff subsequently acquired nine 707-327Cs but switched to DC-8-62s after taking over Panagra in January 1967.

Not previously mentioned U.S. carriers which took delivery of new 707s and/or 720s directly from the manufacturers were Airlift International (2 Model 372Cs), Continental Airlines (5 Model 124s, 2 Pan American-ordered -321Cs, 11 -324Cs, and 8 720-024Bs), Flying Tiger (4 Model 349Cs), Pacific Northern (2 720-062s), Western (5 Model 347Cs and 27 Model 720-047Bs), and World Airways (9 Model 379Cs). In addition, 2 707-355Cs were delivered to Executive Jet Aviation for lease to various airlines, while Saturn Airways, one of the Supplemental Air Carriers, ordered 3 707-379Cs but did not take delivery of these aircraft.

For many of these carriers, the convertible 707-320C became available at the right time, as the U.S. military involvement in Vietnam resulted in defense contracts to carry personnel and non-combat cargo between the United States and bases in Southeast Asia. However, experience showed that when carrying cargo, 707-320Cs often "cubed out" as average freight density

This 720-047B, S/N19208, N3162, sitting on the ramp at LAX in July 1967, in the "good old days" before boarding jetways, was operated by Western Airlines beginning in July 1966. When sold to Wicklund Aviation in January 1980, it was one of the last 720Bs operated by a major carrier. *René J. Francillon*

was relatively low. Accordingly, several of the airlines depending on military contracts and commercial charter operations followed the example of Saturn Airways which, after ordering three 707-379Cs, switched to stretched Douglas DC-8-61CFs which had a more capacious main deck.

The last new 707 delivered to a U.S. airline was a 707-331C (S/N 20429, N794TW) which went to TWA on August 25, 1970 bringing to a close the production history of first generation jetliners for U.S. airlines.

Twenty-eight years later, the 707 era is coming to an end for U.S. carriers, with Boeing reporting that the last nine U.S.-registered 707-320Cs were with Challenge Air Cargo, Grecoair, and Million Air. During the 12-month period ending in June 1998, these nine aircraft had flown a total of only 6.86 hours—less than one half the average daily utilization of a single 707 during the heydays of the type! Typical of these aging jetliners was the ex-Lufthansa 707-330C (S/N 20124, N707HE) of Challenge Air Cargo, which has been retrofitted with upgraded avionics and Comtran hushkits.

## First of the Foreigners

Although Boeing recorded the sale of 10 of its 707-328s to Air France in November 1955, this sale was not announced until February 3, 1956, since domestic political considerations made it

necessary for the French flag carrier to conclude its order for 12 Sud Caravelle Is, the first for the nationally built short- to medium twinjets, prior to publicizing an order for U.S.-built jetliners. The first 707-328 was handed over to Air France on October 21, 1959 and, after initial crew training in Seattle, arrived at Paris-Orly on November 6. The first 707 revenue flight was flown from Orly to Idlewild on January 31, 1960.

The French carrier lost its first 707-328 on July 27, 1961, when S/N17613, F-BHSA, ran off the runway at the Hamburg Airport in Germany after take-off was aborted. Fortunately, there were no fatalities. In subsequent years, Air France lost five additional 707s. Nevertheless, the Boeing jetliner proved otherwise highly satisfactory and, in spite of pressure to favor domestic products, the French airline went on to buy all other types of Boeing jetliners with the notable exception of the 757. Air France operated 38 new-built aircraft (21 -328s, 8 -328Bs, 8 -328Cs, and 1 -355C) and 3 ex-Pan American 707-321Cs acquired in 1976. The last turbojet-powered -328s were sold in 1978. Turbofan-powered 707s lasted another four years with the last passenger revenue flight being provided on October 31, 1982, and the last cargo flight on the very next day.

Having also placed an initial order in November 1955, SABENA took delivery of its first 707-329 on December 4, 1959. During the summer of 1960, shortly after SABENA had placed its first five 707-329s in service, one of these aircraft distinguished itself by flying nonstop from Léopoldville to Brussels, a distance of 3,360 nautical miles (6,223 kilometers), while carrying 301 passengers and crew during an emergency evacuation flight from the newly independent Congo. Unfortunately, a few months later, the Belgian flag carrier gained the unwanted distinction of becoming the first airline to lose a 707 in scheduled service. The aircraft—S/N 17624, OO-SJB, which had been delivered with the short fin but had been modified with the taller vertical surfaces and ventral fin—crashed on approach to Brussels National Airport at the end of a flight from New York on January 15, 1961. The initial contract for JT4A-powered Model 329s was later increased to seven and SABENA went on to acquire seven JT3D-powered -329Cs. By the early eighties, SABENA's remaining turbojet- and turbofan-powered 707s were mostly leased out. The last Belgian 707-329C was sold to the North Atlantic Treaty Organization (NATO) in July 1988.

Unique to Qantas, the turbojet-powered "short body" 707-138 was placed into service when the "down under" carrier inaugurated its Australia to England route, via the Pacific, across the United States, and over the North Atlantic, on September 8, 1959. The more capable turbofan-powered 707-138Bs followed in 1961, and Qantas went on to acquire a total of 34 Boeing 707s from the manufacturer (7 -138s, 6 -138Bs, and 21 -338Cs).

All 37 Conway-powered 707s went to foreign airlines, with the largest operator of this variant being British Overseas Airways Corporation. Placing the type in service on May 27, 1960 on the London–New York route over which its Comet 4s had been outclassed by Pan American 707s, BOAC acquired 16 -436s and ordered 2 more for its subsidiary BOAC-Cunard. It also added 1 -465 delivered to Cunard Eagle Airways and 1 -465 ordered by that carrier but delivered straight to BOAC. The British carrier, which eventually acquired the Cunard's

aviation interest and was reorganized as British Airways in September 1972, also added JT3D-powered Boeing jetliners to its fleet (2 707-336Bs, 2 -336Cs, and 1 -379C).

Notwithstanding claims by vociferous critics which blamed it for not supporting the VC10 adequately, BOAC/British Airways ended up with almost equally sized fleets of 707s and rear-engined VC10s: 20 Conway-powered and 11 JT3D-powered Boeing jetliners (including pre-owned aircraft and aircraft ordered for BOAC-Cunard) versus 12 VC10s and 17 Super VC10s. Contrary facts, however, have seldom deterred politically motivated protagonists from forcefully voicing ill-founded criticisms. British Airways disposed of its last VC10s in 1981 and of its last 707s two years later as 747 jumbo jets fully took over its long-range operations.

Other operators of Conway-powered 707s also later supplemented these aircraft with JT3D-powered 707s and 720Bs. These were Lufthansa (which added 12 -330Bs, 6 -330Cs, and 8 720-030Bs to its 5 Conway 707-430s), Air India (6 Conway -437s, 3 -337Bs, and 2 -337C), VARIG (3 Conway -441s, 3 -341Cs, 3 -345Cs, and 1 -379C, plus numerous pre-owned JT3D-powered 707s), and El Al (3 Conway -458s, 3 -358Bs, 2 -358Cs, and 2 720-058Bs).

Pacific Northern, which acquired a pair of 720-062s, merged with Western Airlines in June 1967. These two JT3C-powered aircraft went to Alaska Airlines in April and May 1973 and were withdrawn from use immediately after being acquired by Pan American in November 1975. *Boeing*

Delivered to SABENA in April 1962, this 707-329 (S/N 18374, OO-SJF) became 4X-JYL with the Israeli Air Force in June 1977. *Boeing*

Previously unmentioned 707 and 720 foreign operators which received aircraft directly from the Renton production line were:

The last 707 built for an airline was S/N 21428, a Model 3F9C accepted by Nigeria Airways on January 30, 1978, nearly 20 years after Pan American had accepted its first 707. True, the de Havilland Comet and the Tupolev Tu-104 had preceded it into service. Equally true, the wide-body 747 has been in production for more years. However, it was the 707 which has had the greatest impact as it heralded sustained jetliner operations for the world's airlines. Since October 26, 1958, when Pan American flew its first 707-121 service, the world has shrunk.

## Pre-Owned

Established 707 and 720 customers began trading delivery positions fairly early in the game in order to build up their jetliner fleet according to traffic demand. That process began when TWA, which had been stymied by Howard Hughes during the initial jetliner buying phase, was forced to release six 707-331 delivery positions, and these aircraft were delivered new to Pan American in 1959–1960. TWA then had to make up for its inadequate fleet by briefly leasing two Northwest Orient Airlines 720-051Bs in 1961–1962 before taking over two World Airways delivery positions for 707-373Cs in 1963.

The number of such transactions between established Boeing operators was, at first, relatively limited. However, when the larger, healthier carriers increased capacity by placing wide-bod-

ied aircraft into service (the 747 in January 1970, the DC-10 in August 1971, the Lockheed TriStar in April 1972, and the A300 in May 1974), Boeing 707s and 720s became available in fast-increasing numbers. At first, most were taken up by established operators which used these "pre-owned" aircraft to build up their fleets at minimum costs. Later on, these first-generation jetliners were more and more frequently acquired by new entrants.

For the 720, the era of "only one careful owner since new" got into stride in the early seventies with these JT3C-powered aircraft being rapidly disposed of by major carriers. The first airline to relinquish its entire fleet of early Boeing jetliners was Eastern Air, which traded its 15 Model 720-025s back to Boeing between September 1969 and June 1970 to acquire more economical 727-225s. United Airlines and Braniff International Airways were next, respectively storing or selling most of their 29 Model 720-022s and 5 -027s in 1973. In that same year, Western Airlines disposed of the 2 720-62s and 1 720-048 it had obtained in its merger with Pacific Northern Airlines. Abroad, the only original 720 customer, Aer Lingus, had been even quicker to dispose of its 3 720-048s, selling one to Pacific Northern and one to British West Indian Airways in 1966, and one to Trans Polar in 1970. American Airlines, which had re-engined its 720-023s with JT3D turbofans, kept most of its 720-023Bs a bit longer, disposing of the last in 1976.

By 1970, 10 Model 707-120s built for air carriers had been lost in accidents, while 35 had been re-engined as -120Bs. Of the remaining 15 JT3C-powered aircraft, 3 707-124s had been sold

| Airline | Number | Model |
|---|---|---|
| Aer Lingus | 4 | -348C |
| | 3 | 720-048 |
| Aerolineas Argentinas | 4 | -387B |
| | 2 | -387C |
| Alia-Royal Jordanian | 2 | -3D3C |
| AVIANCA | 2 | 707-359B |
| | 3 | 720-059B |
| Aviation Services & Support | 1 | -3L6C |
| CAAC | 4 | -3J6B |
| | 6 | -3J6C |
| Caledonian Airways/ | 1 | -365C |
| British Caledonian | 1 | -399C |
| Camair-Air Cameroun | 1 | -3H7C |
| China Airlines | 2 | -309C |
| Eagle Airways | 1 | -365C |
| EgyptAir | 9 | -366C |
| Ethiopian | 1 | -360C |
| | 1 | -379C |
| | 3 | 720-060B |
| Iranair | 4 | -386C |
| Iraqi Airways | 3 | -370C |
| Korean Air | 1 | -3B5C |
| Kuwait Airways | 5 | -369C |
| Libyan Arab Airlines | 1 | -3L5C |
| Malaysian Singapore | 3 | -312B |
| Airlines/Singapore Airline | | |
| Middle East Airlines | 4 | -3B4C |
| Nigeria Airways | 3 | -3F9C |
| Olympic Airways | 2 | -384B |
| | 4 | -384C |
| PIA-Pakistan International | 7 | -340C |
| | 4 | 720-040B |
| Saudia-Saudi Arabian Airlines | 7 | -368C |
| | 2 | 720-068B |
| South African Airways | 3 | -344 |
| | 2 | -344B |
| | 5 | -344C |
| Sudan Air | 2 | -3J8C |
| TAP-Air Portugal | 7 | -382B |
| Tarom | 4 | -3K1C |
| Wardair | 1 | -311C |

by Continental Airlines to TWA in December 1967. In turn, TWA disposed of these aircraft and of its last 12 -131s at the end of 1971. The more capable JT4A- and Conway-powered intercontinental models lasted longer with their original owners. For example, TWA retained some of its 707-331s until the spring of 1979, almost 20 years after this model had entered service. Although during the seventies, British Airways progressively transferred most of its 707-436s to its charter organization, British Airtours, it retained ownership of four Conway-powered aircraft until 1981.

JT3D-powered 707-320Bs and -320Cs remained in production longer than all other 707 and 720 variants. A total of 477 of these aircraft were delivered to airlines between April 1962 and January 1978, with peak deliveries occurring in 1968 when 118 were accepted by carriers. With so many being built for so long, and with their JT3D turbofans proving extremely reliable, it is not surprising that 707-320B/Cs remained in service with most major airlines until the early eighties. Moreover, pre-owned JT3D-powered 707s then quickly found ready customers among smaller carriers, particularly for freight operations.

Early on, most 707s and 720s changing hands went to established Boeing operators, such as Pan American, which expanded its fleet with two ex-Western 707-139s, three ex-American 720-023Bs, and six ex-Lufthansa 720-030Bs. Later transactions, however, increasingly saw pre-owned aircraft being acquired by new jet operators, the first of which was British West Indies Airways, which bought a 720-048 from Aer Lingus in 1966.

Airlines that added pre-owned 707s and/or 720s to their existing fleet of Boeing jetliners were too numerous for details to be provided in this book. Middle East Airlines (MEA) is a good example. Having entered the jet era in April 1963, when it took delivery of the first of three Sud Caravelle VINs, the Lebanese carrier placed an order for three Douglas DC-8-62CFs in February 1966. However, MEA canceled this order nine months later and ordered instead four 707-3B4Cs for delivery starting in November 1968. Moreover, pending delivery of its new Boeing jetliners, it leased a 707-365C from British Eagle for eight months starting in March 1968. Afterward, the Beirut-based airline never again ordered new 707s, as attractively priced aircraft became available from U.S. carriers. Thus, between December 1970 and January 1990, MEA acquired 25 first-generation Boeing jetliners (14 Model 720-023Bs, 4 707-323Cs, and 1 707-323B from American, as well as 4 720-047Bs and 2 707-347Cs from Western).

Sadly, as a result of the protracted conflicts which have torn up Lebanon for most of the past 30 years, MEA had a terrible record with its early Boeing jetliners. While MEA lost 2 707s and 13 720s, 8 of these aircraft were destroyed during Israeli attacks

Illustrated in the markings of the Jet Set Travel Club which leased it in October 1973 and purchased it in November 1978, S/N 18078 is a 720-022 which had been delivered new to United Airlines in April 1962. *Marty Isham*

while 4 were destroyed in "non attributed" airport shelling in which the villains were either Syrian-backed Palestinians or Israeli-supported Lebanese elements. (In this respect, it is worthy to note that no Israeli 707s or 720s, whether civil or military-operated, have been lost. The eight-to-naught record "in favor" of Israel leads one to wonder whether so-called Israel "defense" forces aren't a bit more aggressive than defensive.) The other Lebanese operator of pre-owned 707s, Trans Mediterranean Airways, also lost one of its 11 freighters in a shelling at the Beirut International Airport.

Pre-owned 707s and 720s were acquired not just by scheduled carriers and charter airlines but also by a variety of other customers. Notably, some went to travel organizations (e.g., 720-022 for the Jet Set Travel Club), sport teams (e.g., 720-023B for the Los Angeles Dodgers), government and air forces (as detailed in the next chapter) and to corporations, either as staff transports (e.g., 707-123B for Atlantic Richfield) or as testbeds for engines (e.g., 707-321 for General Electric and 720-023Bs for Pratt & Whitney Canada) and systems (e.g., 720-060B for Hughes Aircraft).

There were also less-legitimate customers, with aircraft being repeatedly leased and sub-leased without the manufacturer having a

Photographed at the Guarulhos International Airport in São Paulo, Brazil, on January 3, 1993, this ex-Pan American 707-321B (S/N 18957, ZP-CCF) has been serving as the presidential aircraft for the Paraguayan government since June 1994. *Ito Noriyuki*

C-FETB, S/N 18024, is an ex-American Airlines 720-023B which after being owned by Middle East Airlines and Aviatek (UK) Ltd., was acquired by Pratt & Whitney Canada Ltd. in December 1985 to be used as an engine testbed. It is seen with a V2500 advanced turbofan in the number 3 position. *Pratt & Whitney Canada, courtesy of Jelle Sjoerdsma*

say in such transactions. Not surprisingly, some of these aircraft ended up being confiscated as the result of their use in drug-smuggling activities. This was notably the case of S/N 20043 which had been ordered as a 707-396C by Quebecair but was delivered to Wardair in March 1969. After nearly ten years of legitimate operations with this Canadian carrier, the aircraft was acquired by Montana Austria. While still owned by this shadowy organization, S/N 20043 was confiscated by the United States Department of Justice in May 1981 and placed in storage at

The number of 707s remaining in airline service is now fast decreasing. Photographed at the Miami International Airport in June 1998, this ex-Qantas, hushkitted 707-338C has been leased by TAMPA Colombia since September 1984. *Kevin Cook*

Davis-Monthan AFB, Arizona, while its fate was determined. Finally, the aircraft returned to respectability after being acquired by the United States Air Force in July 1985 and given the serial number 86-6973 as a C-137C.

## Twilight of the Gods

Notwithstanding the availability of hushkits bringing JT3D-powered 707s into compliance with Stage 2 and Stage 3 noise regulations, the number of civilian operators of early Boeing jetliners is fast dwindling. According to the manufacturer's records, the only carriers still flying 707-320Bs and -320Cs in mid-1998 were based in Azerbaijan (Azerbaijan Hava Yollari), Bolivia (Lloyd Aéreo Boliviano), Brazil (BETA Cargo and Skymaster Airlines), China (China Southwest Airlines), Colombia (TAMPA Colombia), Ecuador (Aries del Sur), Egypt (Air Memphis and EgyptAir), Jordan (Royal Jordanian Airlines), Lebanon (Espace Aviation Services, Middle East Airlines, and Trans Mediterranean Airways), Liberia (Transway Air International), Mexico (Aeropostal de México), Nigeria (Dairo Air Service), Pakistan (PIA), Peru (Servicio Aéreo Ejécutivo), Sudan (Azza Air Transport and Sudan Airways), the United States (Challenge Air Cargo, Grecoair Inc., and Million Air), Zaire (Scibe Airlift), and Zimbabwe (Air Zimbabwe). Together, these operators owned or leased 2 707-320Bs and 58 707-320Cs, but several of these aircraft were only seeing limited use.

# CHAPTER FOUR

# GOVERNMENT OPERATIONS

**D**erivatives of the 367-80 demonstrator operated by air forces and government agencies in the United States and abroad fall into four categories. The first include 820 Model 717s built for the United States Air Force as KC-135 tankers and C-135 transports, and for France's Armée de l'air as C-135Fs. Second, 1 720 and 36 707s were built for the USAF and foreign customers as head-of-state transports, logistic support/staff transport aircraft, and tankers. The third category comprised 93 purpose-built aircraft with what were essentially 707-320B/C airframes and engines, including 68 E-3 airborne early warning and

Previous Page: Air National Guard (ANG) tankers have always been superbly maintained, as evidenced by this KC-135E standing on the sunny ramp of the Salt Lake City International Airport on July 19, 1988. The re-engining of KC-135As with TF33 turbofans was particularly appreciated by Guard units, such as the 191st Air Refueling Squadron, Utah ANG, operating from noise-sensitive civil airports. *René J. Francillon*

control aircraft for the USAF and foreign air forces, 8 KE-3 tankers for the Royal Saudi Air Force, 16 E-6 TACAMO aircraft for the USN, and 1 E-8B built for the USAF but not taken up. Finally, 116 ex-airlines 707s and 720s were acquired by air forces and government organizations as presidential/staff transports or for conversion as military tankers or electronic surveillance platforms. Moreover, the United States Air Force acquired a substantial number of JT3D-powered 707s and 720s from U.S. and foreign airlines to use their turbofans in the re-engining program bringing J57-powered KC-135As up to KC-135E standard and upgrading other J57/JT3C-powered aircraft in various configurations.

## KC-135 and Derivatives

In April 1952, when it initiated development of the 367-80 as a jetliner/jet tanker demonstrator, Boeing lacked an in-depth knowledge of the needs and current operational procedures of the commercial carriers. Conversely, the Seattle manufacturer was the almost undisputed supplier of piston-engined tankers and large jet bombers to the Strategic Air Command (SAC). Its close working relationship with SAC enabled Boeing to anticipate the need for jet tankers to refuel strategic bombers and to have a clearer idea regarding performance requirements and program timing than did competitors with more limited contacts with SAC.

Boeing had gone into the air refueling tanker business in November 1947 when the Air Materiel Command had requested that it study "air-to-air refueling methods & installations." Two months later, on January 20, 1948, Boeing had been asked to submit a cost proposal for design and development of equipment for aerial refueling of piston-engined B-29s and B-50s. While conceptual design work proceeded in Seattle to develop a high-rate-of-flow aerial fuel-transfer system, Boe-

Taken at Edwards AFB in June 1996, this photograph illustrates several of the military applications spawned by the 367-80 flown 42 years earlier. Bearing the Air Force tail number 81-0893, the aircraft in the foreground was built as a 707-323C for American Airlines and is shown here modified as an EC-18D cruise missile mission control aircraft (CMMCA). The prominent nose radome houses an antenna for the telemetry subsystem. Aircraft 55-3135 was delivered to the Air Force as a KC-135A-03-BN in September 1957 and is illustrated as a NKC-135E test aircraft re-engined with TF33-PW-102 turbofans. *USAF/AFFTC*

ing was also asked to install British "looped-hose" refueling equipment provided by Flight Refuelling Limited in specially modified B-29s. Tests with this equipment began in May 1948, and KB-29Ms with looped-hose refueling equipment entered service with two SAC Air Refueling Squadrons in late 1948. Starting in 1950, other B-29s were modified by Boeing to KB-29T standard with the more capable hose-and-drogue system specially developed in Great Britain by Flight Refuelling to refuel probe-equipped USAF jet fighters. However, neither of the British systems could transfer fuel at the high rate required to refuel bombers, particularly jet-powered but fuel-thirsty B-47s due to enter SAC service in 1951.

Boom extended, a KC-135Q of the 9th Strategic Reconnaissance Wing (SRW) prepares to refuel a KC-10A flown by reservists of the 452nd Air Refueling Wing during a training sortie on August 4, 1986. Delivered as a KC-135A-13-BN, 58-0086 was modified to full KC-135Q standard and, re-engined with F108s, remains in USAF service as a KC-135T. *René J. Francillon*

Fortunately, Boeing had in the meantime designed an aerodynamically controlled swiveling and telescoping boom capable of transferring fuel at a satisfactory rate (500 gallons per minute versus a seldom-achieved rate of 200 gallons per minute with the looped-hose system). This flying boom was first tested in October 1948 and boom-equipped KB-29Ps entered SAC service in September 1950.

Capitalizing on its experience with hose-equipped KB-29Ms and boom-equipped KB-29Ps, Boeing next obtained an Air Force contract to modify three of its C-97As into boom-equipped KC-97A tanker prototypes. Successful evaluation of these prototypes led to the award of a contract for 60 KC-97Es, the world's first purpose-built tankers. On July 14, 1951, the first KC-97E was delivered to the 306th Air Refueling Squadron at Mac Dill AFB, Florida, with this squadron being specifically tasked with refueling B-47Bs of the 306th Bombardment Wing. Later, Boeing received additional contracts for KC-97F and KC-97G boom-equipped strategic tankers while Hayes Industries modified 136 obsolescent Boeing B-50s and TB-50s into KB-50J and K three-hose tactical tankers. Piston-powered KB-29s, KB-50s, and KC-97s, however, lacked speed and cruise altitude perfor-

mance to be satisfactory tankers for jet aircraft, particularly heavier and less maneuverable bombers and reconnaissance aircraft such as the North American RB-45 and the Boeing B/RB-47.

The performance deficiency of the Boeing piston-powered tankers and the fact that these aircraft had to carry their gasoline and the jet fuel for the receivers in separate tanks enabled Douglas to challenge the tanker monopoly of its Seattle rival. Taking advantage of this opportunity, Douglas began working in August 1950 on a turboprop-powered tanker using the airframe of its C-124A heavy logistic aircraft.

Powered by four 5,550-horsepower (4,139-kW) Pratt & Whitney YT34-P-1 turboprop engines, the proposed Douglas KC-124B was conceived to refuel jet bombers at a combat speed of 323 knots at 25,000 feet (598 kilometers per hour at 7,620 meters) without having to lose altitude progressively as piston-engined tankers had to do in order to boost speed, because receivers became more difficult to control at lower speeds when weight increased with fuel transfer. Moreover, being turbine-powered, the KC-124B would not have to carry gasoline for its own use and would thus be able to transfer kerosene not only from its specially provided fuselage tanks but also from its standard wing

95

To enable KC-135s to refuel probe-equipped aircraft, Boeing developed a boom drogue adapter (BDA). This BDA is seen on the extended boom of 57-1486, a KC-135R in Air Mobility Command markings. It had originally been delivered as a KC-135A-09-BN in November 1958 and was returned to service in March 1989 after being re-engined. *Author's collection*

tanks. The threat of this interloper, which Douglas aggressively promoted to the Air Force during much of 1951 in competition with Boeing turboprop-powered Model 367-60 and jet-powered Model 367-64 designs, did much to convince the Boeing management to proceed with the development of the 367-80 tanker/jetliner demonstrator.

By the fall of 1953, one year after Boeing had begun cutting metal for the 367-80, SAC had accumulated some 18 months of air refueling experience with B-47s and KC-97s. That length of experience was more than enough to put in evidence the performance shortcomings of piston-engined tankers when refueling jet bombers. Nevertheless, the Air Force was yet to come up with a formal requirement for jet tankers. Heavy military expenditures during the Korean "police action" coming at a time when SAC was making the switch to jet bombers had precluded considering the procurement of jet tankers. However, after the first Stratofortress production contract was finalized in April 1953 (that contract, which initially called for the production of 43 RB-52Bs and was later amended to add 25 RB-52Cs, was finally amended once more to provide for the delivery of these aircraft as bomber-con-

figured B-52Bs and B-52Cs), the need for jet tankers was finally recognized by SAC. Formal consideration of jet tanker requirements was initiated by the Wright Air Development Center on December 14, 1953 and led to the announcement by the Air Force on May 5, 1954 that a design competition would soon start.

Although this announcement vindicated the manufacturer's foresight in initiating the development of the 367-80 some 25 months earlier, it did not guarantee success for the Boeing jet tanker. In fact, on June 18, 1954 (35 days after the 367-80 had been rolled out in Renton but 27 days before its maiden flight), the Air Research and Development Command invited Convair, Douglas, Fairchild, Lockheed, and Martin to join Boeing in participating in the KC-X Jet Tanker/Transport Design Parameter study.

To demonstrate its lead, and hopefully short-circuit the competition, Boeing had a B-52A fly in air-refueling position behind and below the 367-80 during the seventh flight of the tanker/transport demonstrator on July 22, 1954. Although the 367-80 was yet to be fitted with a flying boom and a boom operator's pod (these being added during a lay-up period between June 19 and August 4, 1955), this demonstration was more than a mere publicity stunt as it proved that the 367-80 had the right performance to refuel the Air Force's newest strategic bomber.

Clearly impressed by the July 22 demonstration, and by then having recognized that jet tankers would be needed quickly if early Stratofortresses were to reach initial operational capability soon after entering service, the USAF took the political risk of having Air Force Secretary Harold E. Talbott announce on August 5, 1954 that 29 Boeing Model 717s would be ordered as "interim" jet tankers. Later in the month, and prior to the submissions of proposals in answer to its two-month old KC-X request for proposals, the Air Force ordered 88 additional Boeing "interim" tankers. In spite of these two batches, Boeing was still far from being a shoo-in. Six months later, it was Lockheed which was declared the winner of the KC-X competition. For Lockheed, however, this was a Pyrrhic victory as, in February 1955, only one prototype of the CL-321 was ordered while Boeing was "rewarded" for losing the competition with an additional order for 169 KC-135As, a situation resulting in a lopsided score of winner 1, loser 286!

This "reversed" score not only proved confusing but also was ground for a Congressional perception of favoritism. Accordingly, it led to an inquiry by the Surveys and Investigations Staff of the House Appropriations Committee while consideration was given to canceling both the Lockheed KC-X competition winner and the Boeing "interim" tanker in favor of converting B-36s and/or B-52s as tankers. In the end, however, the technical merits of the KC-135A (concerns were expressed that the twin-engine pods mounted beneath and behind the wings of the Lockheed tanker would generate excessive turbulence rendering station-keeping difficult for receivers) and the earlier availability of the "interim" tanker won the day for Boeing. The contract for the prototype of the Lockheed KC-X winner was never finalized, while a fourth contract for 157 KC-135As was signed on March 27, 1958. Follow-on contracts brought the total of KC-135As ordered by the Air Force to 810, of which 732 were delivered in 27 blocks (KC-135A-01-BN through -27-BN).

Given the designation Model 717 by the manufacturer, the KC-135A differed from the original 367-80 configuration in several major respects. Structurally, it had wings of greater span and area, a fuselage diameter increased from 132 to 144 inches (3.35 to 3.66 meters), only one main-deck cargo door (forward of the wing on the left side), and a strengthened undercarriage. Of course, it was also fitted with a boom operator's station in the lower aft of the fuselage (with the operator lying prone on a couch facing aft and two additional couches being provided for observers or instructors), a flying boom, and additional tankage (including a four-tank forward fuel bay and a five-tank aft fuel

bay beneath the main deck, plus an upper-deck tank aft and above the boom operator's station). It differed from the 707-120 in that its fuselage diameter was 4 inches (10 centimeters) less than the 148 inches (3.76 meters) eventually adopted for the jetliner variants and in that it was built to safe-life requirement with 7178 aluminum alloy instead of fail-safe standard with 2024 alloy. The use of lower strength alloy first led to the need to add 25 external stiffeners on KC-135 rear fuselages to offset sonic fatigue caused by impinging turbojet sound wave and then to a costly wing reskinning program to increase service life from 10,000 to 27,000 hours (still far short from that achieved by 707s, with one of these jetliners having accumulated a total of 92,496 flight hours by mid-1998). Mention must also be made of the fact that taller vertical surfaces were fitted during production beginning with the 583rd C/KC/RC-135 aircraft and were retrofitted to earlier aircraft to improve handling in asymmetric engine conditions.

Rolled out at the Renton plant on July 18, 1956, two years and three days after the maiden flight of the 367-80, the first KC-135A (Boeing S/N 17234, Air Force serial 55-3118) flew on August 31, 1956. Following manufacturer and service trials, which notably confirmed that with J57 engines with military (dry) rating of 11,200 pounds thrust (49.8 kN) and maximum (with water injection) rating of 13,750 pounds thrust (61.2 kN) would most often have to operate at reduced gross weights from the then standard 10,000-foot (3,048-meter) runway at most SAC bases, the KC-135A was declared ready for service use. The first for SAC (55-3127) was delivered to the 93rd Air Refueling

KC-135Qs of the 349th AREFS and 350th AREFS, 9th SRW, are lined up on the tanker ramp at Beale AFB, California, on October 6, 1984. Aircraft 58-0129, which had not yet received its full fin band, was being readied to go on a refueling sortie for the benefit of a Lockheed-operated SR-71A during a post depot maintenance flight. *René J. Francillon*

This front view of a C-135FR of ERV 93 (Air Refueling Squadron 93) *Bretagne*, Armée de l'air, emphasizes recognition points peculiar to French tankers in their latest standard: CFM56 turbofans, Adèle radar warning receiver (with distinctive "bump" above the windshield center post), and wing-mounted Flight Refuelling Mk 32B hose refueling pods. *Christian Jacquet*

Squadron, 93rd Bombardment Wing, at Castle AFB, California, on June 28, 1957. Thereafter the number of KC-135As in service with SAC units grew rapidly, year-end inventory being 24 aircraft in 1957, 182 in 1958, 322 in 1959, 405 in 1960, 444 in 1961, 515 in 1962, and 613 in 1963. Peak SAC jet tanker inventory, 674 aircraft, was reached in 1964 and included a small number of KC-135As modified to refuel Lockheed A-12 and SR-71 high-speed reconnaissance aircraft (the modified aircraft being redesignated KC-135Qs in 1966). The 732nd and last KC-135A, aircraft 64-14840, first flew on December 31, 1964 and was handed over to the Air Force on January 12, 1965. Tankers re-engined as KC-135Es with TF33-PW-102 turbofans entered service with the Air National Guard in July 1982 while KC-135Rs with F108-CF-100 turbofans reached SAC in June 1984.

In addition to boosting considerably SAC's operational capabilities, KC-135As were used during the first 15 months in service to set several world records. The first was set on November 11 and 12, 1957 when aircraft 55-3126 with a crew under the command of General Curtis LeMay, then the Air Force Vice Chief of Staff, flew nonstop from Westover AFB, Massachusetts, to Buenos Aires, Argentina, covering 6,322.85 miles (10,173.5 kilometers) in 13 hours 2 minutes 51 seconds. The more direct return trip to Washington, DC, was flown in 11 hours 3 minutes 57 seconds.

Other records were set on April 7 and 8, 1958 (10,229.3 miles/16,458.9 kilometers nonstop between Tokyo, Japan, and Lajes in the Azores, including a record of 13 hours 45 minutes 46.5 seconds for the Tokyo to Washington, DC, portion of the flight), on June 13, 1958 (Los Angeles to New York in 3 hours 42 minutes 45 seconds), on June 27, 1958 (New York to London in 5 hours 29 minutes 14.6 seconds), on June 29, 1958 (London to New York in 5 hours 53 minutes 12.8 seconds), on July 11, 1958 (Andrews AFB, Maryland, to Hickam AFB, Hawaii, in 11 hours 8 minutes), on September 13, 1958 (Yokota AB, Japan, to Andrews AFB in 12 hours 28 minutes), on September 17, 1958 (five records in a single flight: distance in a closed circuit, 3,125.56 miles/5,029 kilometers; speed over 2,000-kilometers/1,243-mile closed circuit with payloads of 1,000 kilograms/2,205 pounds, 2,000 kilograms/4,409 pounds, 5,000 kilograms/11,023 pounds, and 10,000 kilograms/22,046 pounds); and speed over a 5,000-kilometers/3,108-mile closed circuit, 587.136 miles per hour/944.907 kilometers per hour, without payload and with the previously noted payloads), and on September 24, 1958 (payload of 78,090 pounds/35,421 kilograms to an altitude of 6,562 feet/2,000 meters). Tragically, the June 27, 1958 record attempt between Westover AFB and London by four aircraft was marred by the fatal crash of 56-3599, the first -135 to be lost.

In the tanker role with the USAF, J57-powered KC-135As and KC-135Qs have been phased-out and TF33-powered Guard and Reserve KC-135Es are either being re-engined with F108-CF-100s or phased out. KC-135Rs and KC-135Ts with big fan engines are being upgraded under the Pacer CRAG program with two multi-mission displays, a flight management system, a global positioning system (GPS), and a color weather radar. The modified aircraft, which were re-delivered beginning in the spring of 1998, will remain in service for at least another 20 years, a remarkable achievement for aircraft which have already been in service for some 40 years.

The only other -135s built as tankers were 12 J57-powered aircraft, which were given a C-135F transport designation before being delivered to France in 1964. The 11 survivors were re-engined with CFM56 turbofans as C-135FRs beginning in 1985 and in the past two years have been modified by Boeing in Wichita as three-point tankers with the addition of Flight Refuelling Mk 32B hose refueling pods.

Ex-USAF KC-135As re-engined as KC-135Rs have gone to France's Armée de l'air (three aircraft to supplement 11 C-135FRs beginning in 1996) and Turkey's Türk Hava Kuvvetleri (seven aircraft beginning in 1997). Next to receive ex-USAF tankers are the Republic of Singapore Air Force (four aircraft from 1999) and, probably, the Fuerza Aérea Argentina. Others may well follow.

## Technical Data For the Boeing KC-135A Stratotanker

**Dimensions:** Span 130 feet 10 inches (39.88 meters); length overall 136 feet 2.5 inches (41.52 meters); height 38 feet 4 inches (11.68 meters) with original fin or 41 feet 8.5 inches (12.71 meters) with extended fin; fuselage width 12 feet (3.66 meters); fuselage height 13 feet 10 inches (4.22 meters); wheel base 45 feet 8 inches (13.92 meters); wheel track 22 feet 1 inch (6.73 meters); wing area 2,433 square feet (226 square meters).

**Weights:** Normal take-off weight 261,000 pounds (118,388 kilograms); overload take-off weight 300,800 pounds (136,441 kilograms); typical combat weight 112,400 pounds (50,984 kilograms); maximum landing weight 220,000 pounds (99,790 kilograms).

**Powerplant:** Four Pratt & Whitney J57-P-59W turbojets with maximum thrust rating of 13,750 pounds (61.2 kN), military thrust rating of 11,200 pounds (49.8 kN), and normal rating of 9,500 pounds (42.3 kN). Maximum fuel tank capacity 31,200 U.S. gallons (118,102 liters).

**Accommodation:** Flight crew of five (pilot, copilot, flight engineer, navigator, and boom operator). Maximum cargo load 83,000 pounds (37,650 kilograms) on 5,730 cubic feet (162.25 cubic meters) main deck. Maximum of 80 troops on side-facing canvas seats.

Lined-up with runway 31 at Castle AFB, California, on August 4, 1986, this KC-135A of the 93rd Bombardment Wing was then shared by an operational squadron, the 93rd AREFS, and a training squadron, the 924th AREFS. *René J. Francillon*

**Performance:** Maximum combat speed 519 knots at 30,500 feet (961 kilometers per hour at 9,295 meters); average cruising speed 440 knots (815 kilometers per hour); service ceiling 52,000 feet (15,850 meters); maximum rate of climb at sea level 6,350 feet per minute (32.3 meters/second); typical B-52 buddy refueling combat radius 1,417 nautical miles (2,625 kilometers); maximum ferry range 7,537 nautical miles (13,960 kilometers).

Although given a tanker designation and retaining the boom installation of KC-135As, 17 KC-135Bs had been ordered for SAC as Airborne Command Posts. Powered by TF33-P-5 turbofans, these aircraft were delivered beginning in February 1964 but were redesignated EC-135Cs on January 1, 1965 when three aircraft still remained to be delivered. The last were retired in 1998 when the "Looking Glass" airborne command post mission was transferred to more recent offspring of the 367-80, the Navy E-6B.

Hoping that its tanker/transport demonstrator would also entice the Air Force and/or the Navy (which then had its own Air Transport Wings) to order transport derivatives, Boeing had completed the 367-80 with two main-deck cargo doors, one forward and one aft of the left wing. However, the Navy was unable to fund the acquisition of jet transports, while MATS preferred to await the availability of dedicated jet cargo aircraft in which bulky Army equipment could be more easily loaded. Nevertheless, as an interim solution, Congress approved funding for 50 C-135 jet cargo transports in May 1960. The number of aircraft was later reduced to 45, with the first 15 being delivered between August 1961 and January 1962 as J57-powered C-135As. The last 30 were delivered between February and August 1962 as TF33-powered C-135Bs. In addition, three KC-135As were completed by Boeing to partial C-135A standard, but these "falsies" retained external vestiges of the boom system.

C-135As, the first jet transports for MATS, entered service with the 18th Air Transport Squadron at McGuire AFB, New Jersey, in August 1961. However, these J57-powered proved ill-suited to the task, as their payload/range performance were insufficient and as they required lengthy runways. The TF33-powered C-135Bs did not suffer from these deficiencies, but their loading/unloading remained difficult at all but a few well-equipped bases. Consequently, the C-135As were rapidly modified for other tasks. The C-135Bs lasted longer but, with the exception of aircraft modified as VC-135B for the Special Air Mission (SAM) fleet and as WC-135Bs for the Air Weather Service, were phased out by the Military Airlift Command (which had replaced MATS in January 1966) by 1968.

The USAF also ordered nine J57-powered aircraft as RC-135As for aerial mapping and geodetic survey duties and 10 TF33-powered as RC-135B electronic reconnaissance platforms. Only four RC-135As were delivered between September and December 1965, and on June 14, 1966, after being fitted with its full mapping equipment, aircraft 63-8058 became the last -135 to be flown away from the Boeing plant.

Delivered as a C-135B-04-BN on August 8, 1962, aircraft 62-4138 was modified as a RC-135M in 1967–1968 and as a RC-135W in 1980–1981. It is seen sliding into refueling position below and behind a KC-135A on July 19, 1984. *Carl E. Porter*

By 1972, the RC-135As had outlived their usefulness, and they were converted as KC-135D tankers. The RC-135Bs were completed by Boeing in 1964–1965 without electronic equipment and, on December 30, 1964, aircraft 64-14849 became the last -135 to be rolled out of the assembly line at Renton. All 10 RC-135Bs were flown to Baltimore, where the Glenn L. Martin Company installed SIGINT (Signal Intelligence) equipment and work stations under the "Big Team" conversion program. Redesignated RC-135Cs, the Martin-modified aircraft entered service with the 343rd Strategic Reconnaissance Squadron, 55th Strategic Reconnaissance Wing, at Offutt AFB, Nebraska, in January 1967. Later, two of these aircraft were further modified as RC-135Us while eight became RC-135Vs.

Taxiing at McClellan AFB, California, on March 12, 1974, serial 61-0326 was one of eight C-135As modified as EC-135Ns by the Douglas Aircraft Company in Tulsa, Oklahoma, in 1966–1967. Initially used as an Apollo Range Instrumented Aircraft (ARIA) in support of the U.S. Lunar Exploration Program and then the Skylab space station program, it later served as cruise missile test support aircraft. *Peter B. Lewis*

Space limitations, and the fact that this book is devoted primarily to the 707 and 720 jetliners, prevent providing details on the many post-delivery modifications to aircraft which came out of the Renton plant as KC-135As, KC-135Bs, RC-135As, RC-135Bs, C-135As, C-135Bs, and C-135Fs. In USAF service, modified aircraft were given C, EC, JKC, KC, NC, NKC (including two NKC-135As acquired by the U.S. Navy in 1975 as "King Crow" adversary electronic training platforms), OC, RC, TC, VC, and WC prefixes (with those ending up as ground trainers adding G as the first prefix in their designations) and suffixes from A to Y (with the suffix Z almost certain to be needed in the near future). Readers seeking greater details on the many -135 variants are encouraged to refer to the most authoritative book on the subject: *Boeing KC-135 Stratotanker, More than just a tanker,* authored by Robert S. Hopkins, III, which was published in 1997 by Midland Publishing Limited.

## Military & Government Transports

The modified series number 26 was assigned by Boeing for 707 versions proposed to MATS and layout drawings were prepared between November 1955 and April 1956 for "off-the-shelf" variants of Models 120, 220, and 320 as well as derivatives of the Model 320.

Derivatives of the basic 707-320 were proposed with various combinations of (1) JT4A, JT4B, or JT4C-2W engines, (2) fuselage length reduced from 145 feet 6 inches (44.35 meters) to 137 feet 2 inches (41.80 meters) to compensate for the higher density of military loads by reducing airframe weight, (3) tip tanks, (4) forward main deck cargo door on the left side, (5) modified rear fuselage with clamshell cargo doors and pressure bulkhead swinging down and aft, and (6) vertically hinged tail. Subsequent studies were undertaken under Model 738 designations.

None of these proposals, however, were accepted by the Air Force as, save for ordering the 15 J57-powered C-135As and 30 TF33-powered C-135Bs previously mentioned, the Air Force preferred to await development of a turbofan-powered transport aircraft with high-mounted wings and truckbed height main deck for operations from relatively austere bases lacking cargo loading/unloading facilities. That need was eventually met by the Lockheed C-141A StarLifter, which was declared the winner of the Logistics Transport System 476L design competition in March 1961 and entered service with MATS in April 1965.

For less demanding logistics operations and other government operations, such as transporting heads of state and senior officials, the 707 was in fact better suited than the C-141 and

Flying as Air Force One while carrying President Ford on a primary campaign visit to California, 72-7000 prepares to land at the San Jose Airport, California, on May 25, 1976. Nearly 23 years later, this aircraft was the last of the most prestigious 707s remaining with the 89th Airlift Wing. *Peter B. Lewis*

other specialized military transports. It thus found ready acceptance with some prestigious customers, beginning with the Special Air Mission (SAM) fleet of the United States Air Force, the 1254th Air Transport Wing (ATW) at Andrews AFB.

Given the Air Force designation VC-137A, S/N 17925, serial 58-6970, was the first of three 707-153s for the SAM fleet. It was delivered to Detachment One of the 1258th Air Transport Squadron on May 4, 1959. Like the next two VC-137As, it was provided with a forward VIP compartment with seating for eight, an airborne headquarters in the mid-fuselage, and an aft cabin for 40 passengers. Although not intended as presidential aircraft, that prestigious task still being performed by the piston-engined Lockheed VC-121E and later Douglas VC-118A, the VC-137As were occasionally used by President Eisenhower (first for an official visit to Germany in August 1959) and later by President Kennedy. These three aircraft were redesignated VC-137Bs after being re-engined with TF33 turbofans in 1963. Eventually losing their V prefix, the C-137Bs soldiered into the 1990s, with the last, 58-6971, being retired by the 89th Airlift Wing (AW) in 1997. (The

1254th ATW gave place to the 89th Military Airlift Wing on January 8, 1966, and "Military" was dropped from its designation following the re-organization of the Military Airlift Command into the Air Mobility Command in June 1992.)

The next 707 for the SAM fleet was S/N 18461, serial 62-6000, a 707-353B given the military designation VC-137C, which was delivered as *Air Force One* on October 10, 1962. It originally was fitted with a presidential suite in the rear fuselage and staff accommodation forward. A second VC-137C, 72-7000, was added in December 1972. Both remained with the 89th Airlift Wing in 1998 but had relinquished their assignment as *Air Force One* and *Two* when in September 1990 the first of two VC-25As (specially fitted Boeing 747-2G4Bs) took over the presidential mission and first brought President Bush to a summit meeting in Helsinki, Finland. Two 707s, which had been confiscated from smugglers, have also been given C-137Cs but received more Spartan accommodation. All but one remained assigned to the 89th Airlift Wing until replaced by Boeing C-32As, the exception being 72-7000 which was still with the 89th AW in January 1999.

The USAF has used the EC-137D designation twice for 707 variants, but not for transport-configured aircraft. First, the EC-137D designation was used for the two prototypes of AWACS (Airborne Warning and Control System) as detailed later on. After these two aircraft had been rebuilt as E-3As, the designation was again used for a 707-355C originally built for Executive Jet Aviation and acquired by the Air Force in 1989. Modified by E-Systems as an electronic support aircraft, 67-19417 was still with the 2nd Special Operations Flight, Air Force Special Operations Command (AFSOC) in 1998. In 1982, the Air Force also acquired eight ex-American Airlines 707-323Cs which were initially given C-18As designations. Six of these aircraft were later fitted with a telemetry reception antenna in an oversized nose radome, four becoming EC-18B advanced range instrumentation aircraft (ARIAs) and two EC-18D cruise missile mission control aircraft (CMMCAs). Two ex-TWA 707-331Cs became TC-18E "bounce bird" trainers for E-3 pilots, while the Navy obtained two ex-Air Portugal 707-382Bs as TC-18F trainers for its E-6 pilots.

Foreign air forces and governments which ordered new transport-configured 707s from Boeing were those of Argentina (one 707-387B), Canada (five -347Cs including two later modified as tanker/transports), Egypt (one -366C), Germany (four -307Cs), Iran (one -386C plus 14 tanker/transports described later on), Libya (one -3L5C), Portugal (two -3F5Cs), Qatar (one -3P1C), and Saudi Arabia (one -368C).

Ex-airlines 707s were acquired for transport use by the governments of Angola (one 707-3J6B modified by Israeli Aircraft Industries, IAI, as a head-of-state transport), Argentina (two -387Bs, one -365C, and two -372Cs plus a -387C later modified as an ELINT/SIGINT platform), Australia (three -368C transports, one -368C only used for spare parts, and four -338C tanker/transports), Benin (one -321 and one 336B), Chile (one 321B and one -351C, plus one -385C later modified by IAI as an airborne early warning aircraft), Indonesia (one -3M1C), Iran (one -370C), Israel (three -124s, three -131s plus two leased -131s, one -321, five -328s, one -328B, three 329s, two -331Cs, two -344Cs, one -3H7C, one -3J6B, one -3J6C, and one 3L6C—modifications to these aircraft are detailed under the next heading), Liberia (one -321B and one 351B/SCD), Morocco (one -138B and one -3W8C later modified as a tanker/transport), NATO (three -329Cs as TCAs, trainer/cargo aircraft), Pakistan (one -340C and one -351B), Paraguay (one -321B), Peru (two -351Cs and one -358C plus one -323C modified by IAI as a tanker/transport), Qatar (one -336C), Saudi Arabia (one -138B and one -368C), South Africa (one -344C), Spain (one -331B plus one -331C and one -368C as tanker/transports), Sudan (one -368C), United Arab Emirates (one -3L6B for Abu Dhabi and one -3L6C for Dubai), and Zaire (one -382B).

Whether acquired new or pre-owned, most military/government 707s remain in service. That is not the case for the only two 720s acquired by foreign governments. S/N 18351, an ex-Northwest Orient Airlines 720-051B which had been acquired in 1971 by Taiwan as a transport for President Chiang Kai-shek, was withdrawn in 1991. S/N 19523, an ex-Western Airlines 720-047B which was bought by the Togo Government in November 1980, was sold in March 1983.

The first 707 tanker was S/N 19000, a -385C convertible passenger/cargo jetliner built for American Flyers, which Boeing equipped with Beech Model 1800 refueling pods mounted directly under the wingtips. Later conversions carried their refueling pods slightly more inboard. *Boeing*

Coded 5-241, the first 707-3J9C tanker built for the Imperial Iranian Air Force was completed only with a refueling boom. It was later retrofitted with Beech wing pods as seen in this view. The receiver is an ex-TWA 707-131 retrofitted with a boom receptacle by Boeing Military Airplane Company in Wichita, Kansas. *Boeing*

## Tankers & Electronic Warfare Platforms

After the last KC-135As were delivered in December 1964, Boeing was left without a jet tanker at a time when it expected to receive foreign orders for tankers. Accordingly, in 1965, the company decided to modify an unsold 707-385C (S/N 19000, which had been ordered by American Flyers but was not taken up) as a tanker demonstrator. As the USAF then was the only air force with aircraft fitted with a receptacle for boom refueling, the 707 demonstrator was fitted with Beech 1800 pods mounted under the wingtips and containing a short hinged boom and trailing hose and drogue. Even though the modification proved successful, Boeing was initially unable to secure orders for 707 tankers and, after the refueling pods and related equipment had been removed, S/N 19000 was delivered to LAN-Chile as a straight jetliner in December 1969.

No sooner had this aircraft been sold as a jetliner than orders for tankers finally materialized. The first was from the Canadian Armed Forces, which requested that two of its five 707-347Cs (which were given the Canadian military designation of CC-137) ordered for delivery in 1970–1971 be given provision for carrying Beech refueling pods. Next came an order from the Imperial Iranian Air Force for 14 707-3J9C tankers. The first six were delivered

with a flying boom to refuel IIAF F-4 Phantom IIs and pre-owned 747s which had been fitted with a refueling receptacle by Boeing Military Airplanes in Wichita. These six boom tankers were later retrofitted with Beech refueling pods beneath the wings while the next eight were delivered with both the boom and the pods installed during production. Eight tankers for the Royal Saudi Air Force (RSAF) were similarly equipped but were CFM56-powered KE-3As with airframes and systems similar to those of Saudi E-3A airborne early warning and control aircraft. Handed over to the RSAF on September 16, 1987, KE-3A serial 1815 (S/N 23426) became the last of 24 new-built 707 tankers delivered by Boeing.

As a less expensive alternative to new-built tankers, Boeing also marketed jetliner conversions to two- and three-hose-and-drogue tanker configurations. To serve as a demonstrator, Boeing leased a 707-331C (S/N 18757, N792TW) from TWA in October 1982 and purchased it 25 months later. While on lease, this

Information regarding 707s in service with the Heyl Ha'Avir are conflicting. Photographed at the Orly Airport in Paris, 4X-JYQ, S/N 20110, is an ex-South African Airways 707-344C. Antennas above the rear fuselage indicate that this transport may double up as an airborne command post or as a SIGINT platform. *Jacques Guillem*

Initially, Boeing proposed that its AWACS be powered by eight General Electric TF34-GE-2 turbofans in paired nacelles as shown in this artist's rendering. *Boeing*

aircraft was fitted with a Sargent-Fletcher Model 34-000 hose reel pod beneath each wing and a FR 600B hose reel under the rear fuselage centerline. With the centerline reel deleted, this aircraft was delivered in November 1988 to Spain's Ejército del Aire. In Spanish service, this aircraft was followed by a second Boeing tanker conversion in 1990 and by an Israeli-modified tanker/ELINT aircraft in 1996. Boeing also converted four 707s for Brazil's Força Aérea Brasileira but fitted them with Beech wing refueling pods. Finally, Boeing assisted AMIN Maroc Aviation in fitting Flight Refuelling Limited (FRL) wing pods to the 707-3W6C (ex 707-700 prototype) of Morocco's Al Quwwat al Jawwiya al Malakiya Marakishiya and Alenia Officine Aeronavali in installing Sargent-Fletcher wing and centerline reels on four 707s for Italy's Aeronautica Militare Italiana.

The story of Israeli tankers is more nebulous due to the obsession with security on the part of *Zahal* censors. What is known is that, in addition to leasing briefly two 707-131s from IAI to boost its airlift capability during the 1973 Yom Kippur War, the Heyl'Avir acquired 24 JT3C-, JT4A-, and JT3D-powered 707s (see list under the Military & Government Transports heading). The Sargent-Fletcher Company also reported that it delivered 7 sub-systems (14 Model 34-000 pods and 7 FR 300K centerline hose reels) to IAI and that it worked on this program between March 1983 and April 1985. For its part, IAI has openly marketed 707 tanker conversions with Sargent-Fletcher or Flight Refuelling wing pods and either a fuselage reel or an IAI flying boom.

In landing configuration, this E-3B of the 963rd Airborne Warning and Control Squadron shows off the modified trailing edge of its engine pylons in which are faired "Have Siren" infrared jammers. *René J. Francillon*

The Israeli-developed boom is quite similar to that from Boeing, but the operator controls the boom from a station inside the rear fuselage by means of a remote-control TV camera system, instead of from a station beneath the rear fuselage with direct view of the receiver. On tanker conversions by IAI's Bedek Aviation Group/Aircraft Division, refueling pods—either Sargent-Fletcher or Flight Refuelling Mk 32B—are mounted further from the wingtips than on Boeing conversions.

Although the Boeing list of active aircraft dated June 30, 1998 still included one unidentified JT3C-powered 707 (4X-JYE) and one 707-329 (S/N17625, 4X-JYT, said to have logged 0.46 hours in the previous 12 months), it is believed that only nine JT3D-powered 707s (two -320Bs and seven -320Cs) remain operational with the Heyl Ha'Avir. These nine military 707s include transport-configured aircraft given the Hebrew name of R'em (Unicorn), Saknayee (Pelican) tankers, Chasidah (Stork) ELINT aircraft, and Barboor (Swan) SIG-INT/COMINT-configured platforms.

In addition to converting 707s for the national air force, IAI Bedek has fitted hose reels to a 707-330B tanker for the Fuerza Aérea de Chile, a 707-373C for the Fuerza Aérea Colombiana, and a 707-323C for the Fuerza Aérea del Peru. It fitted both Sargent-Fletcher pods and an IAI boom to two 707-384Cs for the Fuerza Aérea Venezolana. Four tankers for the South African Air Force (SAAF) received Flight Refuelling wing pods and centerline unit while another SAAF tanker dispenses with the centerline unit but has ELINT equipment in a fairing on both sides of the forward fuselage.

So far, a third prospective supplier of tanker conversions, the team Omega Air and Tracor Flight Systems, has remained unsuccessful. Its demonstrator was obtained by fitting a centerline hose reel unit in a CC-137 (707-347C) phased out by the Canadian Forces in December 1993.

Whether built by Boeing, modified by either Boeing or IAI, or modified by others with Boeing or IAI assistance, 707 tankers are in service with 14 air forces as listed below:

Mentions has been made of 707s converted by IAI Bedek as COMINT/ELINT/SIGINT platforms for Israel's Heyl Ha'Avir and for export customers (one 707-387C for the Fuerza Aérea Argentina, one -328C for the South African Air Force, and one -351C for the Ejército del Aire Español). Other electronic warfare conversions include a Saudi KE-3A (serial 1817) which may have been redesignated KE-3B after booms and refueling pods gave place to electronic cheeks and an "antenna farm" underneath the fuselage as part of a modification program undertaken by E-Systems. In India, a 707-337B and a -327C have been modified by Hindustan Aeronautics Limited as ELINT/COMINT platforms for the Bharatiya Vayu Sena.

| Country | Number of Aircraft | Contractor | Wing Pods | Centerline Hose Reel | Boom |
|---|---|---|---|---|---|
| Australia | 4 | ASTA/IAI | FRL | N/A | N/A |
| Brazil | 4 | Boeing | Beech | N/A | N/A |
| Canada | 2 | Boeing | Beech | N/A | N/A |
| Chile | 1 | IAI | FRL | N/A (or FRL ?) | N/A |
| Colombia | 1 | IAI | FRL | N/A | N/A |
| Iran | 14 | Boeing | Beech | N/A | Boeing |
| Israel | N/A | IAI | S-F | S-F | N/A |
|  | N/A | IAI | S-F or FRL | N/A | IAI |
| Italy | 4 | Boeing/Alenia | S-F | S-F | N/A |
| Morocco | 1 | AMIN | Beech | N/A | N/A |
| Peru | 1 | IAI | FRL | N/A | N/A |
| Saudi Arabia | 8 | Boeing | Beech | N/A | Boeing |
| South Africa | 4 | IAI | FRL | FRL | N/A |
|  | 1 | IAI | FRL | None (ELINT) | N/A |
| Spain | 2 | Boeing | S-F | N/A | N/A |
|  | 1 | IAI | S-F | None (ELINT) | N/A |
| Venezuela | 2 | IAI | S-F | N/A | IAI |

## AWACS & Joint STARS

After the issuance of a Specific Operational Requirement on June 12, 1963, a protracted competition pitted Boeing against Lockheed and McDonnell Douglas to provide the Air Force with an Airborne Warning and Control System based respectively on their 707-320B, C-141A, and DC-8-62. By the time the Air Force was ready to select a contractor, the C-141 was no longer in production and McDonnell Douglas appeared less than committed to continuing DC-8 production to concentrate on that of its wide-body DC-10. Not surprisingly, Boeing was selected in June 1970.

Initially proposed with eight 9,065 pounds thrust (40.3 kN) General Electric TF34-GE-2 turbofans in twin nacelles, two prototypes were powered by four TF33s. Given the EC-137D designation, they were intended as development platforms for competing Hughes and Westinghouse pulse Doppler radar with antenna in a strut-mounted rotodome above the rear fuselage. Aircraft 71-1407 and 71-1408 first flew at Renton one day apart on February 9 and 10, 1972. The Westinghouse AN/APY-1 radar was selected on October 5, 1972 for the production AWACS platform given the E-3 designation. The two

EC-137Ds were rebuilt as E-3As and the first production E-3A, serial 73-1674, flew on July 21, 1975 without its AN/APY-1 and on October 31, 1975 with full systems installed. Deliveries to the 552nd Airborne Warning and Control Wing (AWCW) at Tinker AFB, Oklahoma, began in March 1977, with the 552nd AWCW achieving initial operational capability in April 1978.

Including the two ex-EC-137Ds, Boeing built a total of 52 TF33-powered E-3s. Twenty-three new aircraft and the two rebuilt EC-137Ds were delivered to the USAF as E-3As in "core configuration" with AN/APY-1 radar, IFF/TADIL (Identification Friend or Foe/Tactical Digital Information Link), CC-1 high-speed computer, and nine situation display consoles. Nine E-3As for the USAF and 18 E-3As for NATO were delivered in "standard configuration" with AN/APY-2 radar incorporating full maritime surveillance capability, CC-2 computer, 14 situation display consoles, and 12 instead of seven UHF radios.

The NATO E-3As entered service with the multi-national Airborne Early Warning and Control (AEW&C) Force based at Geilenkirchen, Germany, in 1982. The E-3B designation identified the two ex-EC-137Ds and 22 other "core configuration" E-3As upgraded for the USAF to the "standard configuration,"

The E-8C achieved initial operational capability (IOC) with the 93rd Air Control Wing in December 1997. In the years preceding IOC for the Joint STARS, the two E-8As had been used operationally during Desert Storm in 1991, an E-8A and an E-8C supported Operation Joint Endeavor in Bosnia-Herzegovina between December 1995 and March 1996, and E-8Cs again took part in Operation Joint Endeavor beginning in 1996–1997. *Jim Dunn*

while the E-3C designation identified USAF E-3As (one in "core" and nine in "standard" configurations) retrofitted with "Have Quick" A-NETS secure communication system and other classified equipment. More recent upgrades have resulted in the addition of the "Quick Look" electronic support measures (ESM) system in undernose and forward fuselage side fairings and of TADIL/JTIDS (Tactical Digital Information Link/Joint Tactical Information Distribution System).

## Technical Data For the Boeing E-3C Sentry

**Dimensions:** Span 145 feet 9 inches (44.42 meters); length overall 152 feet 11 inches (46.61 meters); height 41 feet 9 inches (12.73 meters); fuselage width 12 feet 4 inches (3.76 meters); wheel base 59 feet (17.98 meters); wheel track 22 feet 1 inch (6.73 meters); wing area 2,892 square feet (268.7 square meters).

**Weights:** Empty weight 174,076 pounds (78,960 kilograms); typical combat weight 210,250 pounds (95,368 kilograms); maximum take-off weight 325,000 pounds (147,418 kilograms); maximum landing weight 220,000 pounds (99,790 kilograms).

**Powerplant:** Four Pratt & Whitney TF33-PW-100A turbofans

with maximum thrust rating of 21,000 pounds (93.4 kN). Maximum fuel tank capacity 22,910 U.S. gallons (86,722 liters).

**Accommodation:** Flight crew of four (pilot, copilot, flight engineer, and navigator) and mission crew of 16.

**Performance:** Maximum combat speed 473 knots at 23,400 feet (876 kilometers per hour at 7,130 meters); average cruising speed 420 knots (778 kilometers per hour); station altitude 29,000 feet (8,840 meters); service ceiling 34,400 feet (10,485 meters); maximum rate of climb at sea level and combat weight 4,520 feet per minute (22.9 meters/second); time on station at 600 nautical miles (1,110 kilometers) from base 7.4 hours unrefueled and 16.1 hours with one KC-135 refuel; maximum ferry range 4,290 nautical miles (7,945 kilometers).

For export customers, AWACS platforms have been built with 24,000 pounds thrust (106.8 kN) CFM International CFM56-2A-2 and -2A-3 turbofans. The first five were "standard configuration" E-3As for the Royal Saudi Air Force, with deliveries for service with the No. 18 Squadron at the Riyadh Military Air Base being made between June 1986 and September 1987.

Homeported at Tinker AFB, Oklahoma, since September 1992, the "Iron Men" of VQ-3 maintain an E-6A detachment at Travis AFB, California, where BuNo 164387 was photographed on May 6, 1993. *René J. Francillon*

The dorsal radome of this E-6B house a MILSTAR antenna. For communications with submerged submarines, a long trailing wire antenna (LTWA) is deployed from beneath the rear fuselage while a short trailing wire antenna (STWA) is deployed from the aft cone. Electronic support measures gear is housed in wingtip pods with HF antenna protruding forward from a mast beneath the ESM pods. *Renato E. F. Jones*

Seven E-3Ds, given the Sentry AEW Mk 1 designation in British service, were delivered to the Royal Air Force (RAF) between March 1991 and May 28, 1992 (when serial ZH107, S/N 24499, became the last 707/720 aircraft to be handed over to a customer—almost 34 years after Pan American had taken title to S/N 17588 on August 15, 1958). The RAF Sentries differed from the similarly powered Saudi E-3As in having their boom receptacle supplemented by a fixed refueling probe for compatibility with British VC10 and Tristar tankers and in being fitted with British equipment, including wingtip-mounted Loral 1017 "Yellow Gate" ESM pods. Four nearly identical E-3Fs with ESD (Electronic Systems Division) "Adèle" radar warning receivers replacing "Yellow Gate" ESM, were delivered to France's Armée de l'air between May 1991 and February 1992.

The IAI Phalcon (Falcon) is another 707 airborne early warning platform developed in Israel by Elta Electronics Industries with EL/M-2075 phased-array radar with six conformal antennas. Four of these L-band fixed antenna arrays are located in pairs on each side of the fuselage, fore and aft of the wings; one is in an enlarged nose radome; and one is mounted under the tail. In addition to the radar, the Phalcon is provided with an Elta EL/L-8312 ESM system with narrow- and wide-band receivers and a high-gain directional antenna. The cockpit crew is supplemented by a mission commander and 12 systems operators.

Although there have been apparently unfounded rumors that Israel's Heyl Ha'Avir acquired one or more aircraft given the Hebrew name of Tavas (Peacock), the only aircraft confirmed to have been modified by IAI to the Phalcon configuration is S/N 19000, the aircraft which Boeing had used in 1968 as its first 707 tanker demonstrator. Delivered to LAN-Chile as a standard 707-385C jetliner in December 1969, this aircraft was acquired by the Fuerza Aérea de Chile in January 1991, and was operated as a military transport until sent to IAI for conversion. After being modified to Phalcon standard, this aircraft first flew in its new

The 720 only saw limited paramilitary service. S/N 18158, an ex-Eastern Air 720-025, was modified by Boeing in 1972 to serve as an antisubmarine warfare (ASW) test aircraft in support of a 707-320C derivative which was proposed, unsuccessfully, to the Canadian Armed Forces for use in the maritime patrol role. *Boeing*

configuration on May 12, 1953. It was re-delivered to the Fuerza Aérea de Chile two years later.

Whereas in 1970 the USAF had elected to have its AWACS use new-built airframes, 22 years later it decided to have the equally complex and costly Joint Air Force/Army Surveillance Target Attack Radar System (Joint STARS) developed around pre-owned 707s.

In November 1985, after ten years of research, the Melbourne Systems Division of Grumman Corporation won a $657 million Air Force contract to install Joint STARS prototype systems in two 707s, including an AN/APY-3 radar jointly developed by Grumman and Norden Systems to alternate between SAR (synthetic aperture) and Doppler modes. Grumman then awarded a $80.2 million subcontract to Boeing Military Airplane Company to have two pre-owned 707 jetliners, an ex-Qantas -338C and an ex-American Airlines -323C, overhauled and fitted with a strengthened main deck and an aerial refueling receptacle. Initially designated EC-18Cs, these two aircraft were redesignated E-8As before being delivered to the

Grumman facility in Melbourne, Florida, for installation of mission equipment. The first flight in full Joint STARS configuration was made in Florida on December 22, 1988. While still under test, the two E-8A Joint STARS demonstrators were deployed to Saudi Arabia and proved invaluable during the Gulf War in January and February of 1991.

On the strength of this performance, the decision was made in 1992 to proceed with the program. However, instead of installing mission equipment in 22 new-built E-8Bs powered by CFM F108 engines, cost cutting considerations forced the Department of Defense to have pre-owned 707s upgraded to the E-8C Joint STARS configuration. Boeing, which had flown a first E-8B on December 7, 1990, dropped out of the Joint STARS program.

Designated E-8Cs, Joint STARS production airframes are 707-320C jetliners remanufactured at Northrop Grumman's Louisiana Operations in Lake Charles. The electronics are installed and tested in the modified aircraft by Northrop Grumman in its Integration and Test Facility in Melbourne, Florida.

The first E-8C flew on March 25, 1994. Assigned to the 93rd Air Control Wing at Robins AFB, Georgia, the E-8C Joint STARS reached initial operational capability in December 1997. The program has been downsized, and currently the Air Force is scheduled to receive its 13th and last E-8C in the year 2003. Export orders remain a possibility, and it is likely than the E-8Cs, as well as the two E-8As which are to be brought up to E-8C standard with 18 instead of 10 operator consoles, will be re-engined eventually, alongside USAF E-3B/Cs, with CFM F108 turbofans.

## TACAMO & Antisubmarine Warfare (ASW)

In 1983, the Navy elected to replace the turboprop-powered Lockheed EC-130Qs providing national command authorities with the means to communicate with submerged nuclear-powered ballistic missile submarines (SSBNs) with new-built 707-320Cs. To be powered by CFM F108 turbofans, these airframes were to be fitted with the TACAMO IV equipment to be removed from the EC-130Qs.

The first E-6A flew at Renton on February 19, 1987 before being fitted with TACAMO equipment. After this had been installed, BuNo 162782 was returned to flight status in June 1987. Delivery to Fleet Air Reconnaissance Squadron Three (VQ-3) at NAS Barbers Point, Hawaii, began in August 1989. However, the first operational mission was not flown until October 1993, some 22 months after the 16th and last E-6A had been accepted by the U.S. Navy.

With the reduction in nuclear threat and the resulting downsizing of military forces, the need to maintain both Air Force-manned National Emergency Airborne Command Post (NEACP) EC-135Cs and Navy TACAMO E-6As became difficult to justify. As the E-6As are newer, more capacious, and more economical to operate than the EC-135Cs, the Department of Defense decided to phase out the elderly Air Force aircraft and to transfer the "Looking Glass" mission to the Navy. To that end, Chrysler Technologies Airborne Systems Inc. (CTAS) in Waco, Texas, was chosen to bring the E-6As to the E-3B configuration under the Avionics Block Upgrade (ABU).

Included in this ABU was the installation of the extremely high frequency (EHF) MILSTAR satellite communications equipment removed from the EC-135Cs and housed in a distinctive radome above the fuselage. Evaluation of the first ABU-modified E-6B, BuNo 164406, which had been delivered to the Navy as an E-6A in April 1991, commenced during the summer of 1994. E-6Bs are now fully operational with two squadrons of Strategic Communications Wing One (VQ-3 and VQ-4) home-ported as a tenant unit at Tinker AFB, Oklahoma.

## Technical Data For the Boeing E-6A Mercury

**Dimensions:** Span 148 feet 2 inches (45.16 meters); length overall 152 feet 11 inches (46.61 meters); height 42 feet 5 inches (12.93 meters); fuselage width 12 feet 4 inches (3.76 meters); wheel base 59 feet (17.98 meters); wheel track 22 feet 1 inch (6.73 meters); wing area 3,050 square feet (283.35 square meters).

**Weights:** Operating weight empty 172,295 pounds (78,378 kilograms); maximum take-off weight 342,000 pounds (155,128 kilograms).

**Powerplant:** Four CFM International F108-CF-100 turbofans with maximum thrust rating of 24,000 pounds (106.8 kN). Maximum fuel tank capacity 26,462 U.S. gallons (100,167 liters).

**Accommodation:** Flight crew of four (pilot, copilot, flight engineer, and navigator) and mission crew of seven.

**Performance:** Maximum combat speed 530 knots at 30,000 feet (981 kilometers per hour at 9,150 meters); typical cruising speed 455 knots (843 kilometers per hour); normal operating altitude 25,000 to 30,000 feet (7,620 to 9,150 meters); service ceiling 42,000 feet (12,800 meters); unrefueled endurance at 1,000 nautical miles (1,850 kilometers) from base 10.5 hours.

At the beginning of the 1970s, having just sold five 707-347Cs to the Canadian Armed Forces for use as transports and tanker/transports, Boeing felt that it had a fair chance to have a derivative of its 707-320C selected by Canada as a replacement for Canadair CP-107 Argus maritime patrol aircraft with which Nos. 404, 405, and 415 Squadrons were equipped.

To obtain a demonstrator of its proposed maritime patrol aircraft at minimum cost, Boeing elected to modify an ex-Eastern Air 720-025 which it had been forced to repossess from its second owner, Trans Polar, in May 1971. Re-registered N3183B, S/N 18158 was fitted by Boeing Military Airplane Company with magnetic anomaly detection (MAD) booms on both wingtips, search radar beneath the forward fuselage, and other antisubmarine systems in the fuselage to serve as a systems testbed for the proposed 707-320C antisubmarine warfare (ASW) derivative. In this form, the Boeing ASW Test aircraft first flew at Wichita, Kansas, on April 6, 1972. Competing against entries from six North American and European manufacturers, the 707-320C proposal made it as one of the two finalists in the Canadian competition. In the end, however, it was the Lockheed CP-140 Aurora, a Canadianized version of the P-3 Orion, which was selected by the Canadian Armed Forces in November 1975. Work on 707 ASW derivatives was terminated.

# APPENDIX

## APPENDIX 1: ATTRITIONS

| Date | Model | Registration | Operator | Location | Circumstance |
|------|-------|--------------|----------|----------|--------------|
| Aug 15, 1959 | 707-123 | N7514A | American Airlines | Near Calverton, New York | Crashed during training flight |
| Oct 19, 1959 | 707-227 | N707R | Braniff Airways | Arlington, Washington | Crashed during acceptance flight |
| Jan 15, 1961 | 707-329 | OO-SJB | SABENA | Brussels National AP, Belgium | Crashed on approach |
| Jan 28, 1961 | 707-123 | N7502A | American Airlines | Near Montauk, New York | Crashed |
| Jul 27, 1961 | 707-328 | F-BHSA | Air France | Fuhlsbüttel AP, Hamburg, Germany | Destroyed in aborted take-off |
| Dec 4, 1961 | 720-030B | D-ABOK | Lufthansa | Near Ebersheim, Germany | Crashed |
| Mar 1, 1962 | 707-123 | N7506A | American Airlines | Jamaica Bay, New York | Crashed into bay |
| May 22, 1962 | 707-124 | N70775 | Continental Airlines | Centerville, Iowa | Inflight explosion due to sabotage |
| Jun 3, 1962 | 707-328 | F-BHSM | Air France | Paris-Orly AP, France | Damaged beyond repair in aborted take-off |
| Jun 22, 1962 | 707-437 | VT-DJJ | Air India | Bombay AP, India | Damaged beyond repair |
| Nov 27, 1962 | 707-441 | PP-VJB | VARIG | Near Lima, Peru | Crashed |
| Feb 12, 1963 | 720-051B | N724US | Northwest Orient | Everglades, Florida | Crashed |
| Dec 8, 1963 | 707-121 | N709PA | Pan American | Elkton, Maryland | Crashed |
| Apr 7, 1964 | 707-139 | N779PA | Pan American | JFK IAP, New York | Damaged beyond repair after overrunning runway |
| Jul 15, 1964 | 720-030B | D-ABOP | Lufthansa | Near Ansbach, Germany | Crashed during training flight |
| Nov 23, 1964 | 707-331 | N772TW | TWA | Rome-Fiumicino AP, Italy | Damaged beyond repair in aborted take-off |
| May 20, 1965 | 720-040B | AP-AMH | PIA | Near Cairo, Egypt | Crashed |
| Jul 1, 1965 | 707-124 | N70773 | Continental Airlines | Kansas City IAP, Missouri | Crashed on landing |
| Sep 17, 1965 | 707-121 | N708PA | Pan American | Chances Mountain, Antigua | Crashed into mountain |
| Jan 24, 1966 | 707-437 | VT-DMN | Air India | Mont Blanc, France | Crashed into mountain during descent toward Geneva-Cointrin AP, Switzerland |
| Mar 5, 1966 | 707-436 | G-APFE | BOAC | Mount Fuji, Japan | Crashed into mountain |
| Nov 6, 1967 | 707-131 | N742TW | TWA | Cincinnati, Ohio | Damaged beyond repair |
| Jan 9, 1968 | 720-060B | ET-AAG | Ethiopian Airlines | Beirut IAP, Lebanon | Destroyed by fire in landing accident |
| Feb 7, 1968 | 707-138 | VH-EBC | Qantas | Vancouver IAP, British Colombia, Canada | Damaged beyond repair while landing |
| Mar 5, 1968 | 707-328C | F-BLCJ | Air France | Near Pointe-à-Pitre, Guadeloupe Antilles | Crashed into mountain |
| Apr 8, 1968 | 707-465 | G-ARWE | BOAC | London-Heathrow, England | Ground fire |
| Apr 20, 1968 | 707-344C | ZS-EUW | South African Airways | Windhoek, South Africa | Crashed shortly after take-off |
| Jun 12, 1968 | 707-321C | N798PA | Pan American | Calcutta, India | Crashed on landing |
| Jul 13, 1968 | 707-329C | OO-SJK | SABENA | Near Lagos, Nigeria | Crashed |
| Sep 7, 1968 | 707-341C | PP-VJR | VARIG | Galeão IAP, Rio de Janeiro, Brazil | Ground fire |
| Dec 12, 1968 | 707-321B | N494PA | Pan American | Off Caracas, Venezuela | Crashed into sea |
| Dec 26, 1968 | 707-321C | N799PA | Pan American | Elmendorf AFB, Alaska | Crashed on take-off |
| Dec 28, 1968 | 707-3B4C | OD-AFC | MEA | Beirut IAP | Destroyed by Israeli commandos |
| Jul 26, 1969 | 707-331C | N787TW | TWA | Pomona, New Jersey | Crashed |
| Dec 4, 1969 | 707-328B | F-BHSZ | Air France | Off Venezuelan coast | Crashed after taking-off from Caracas |
| Apr 22, 1970 | 707-131 | N743TW | TWA | Indianapolis, Indiana | Ground fire |
| Sep 13, 1970 | 707-331B | N8715T | TWA | El Khana, Jordan | Blown up on the ground by terrorists |
| Nov 30, 1970 | 707-373C | N790TW | TWA | Lod IAP, Tel Aviv, Israel | Take-off accident |
| Jan 23, 1971 | 707-437 | VT-DJI | Air India | Bombay AP, India | Overran runway |

Pakistan International Airlines lost one of the four 720-040Bs it had ordered from Boeing on May 20, 1965 and, on January 8, 1981, an ex-Western Airlines 720-047B which it had acquired from Itel Corporation. *Boeing*

| Date | Model | Registration | Operator | Location | Circumstance |
|------|-------|-------------|----------|----------|--------------|
| Mar 31, 1971 | 720-047B | N3166 | Western Airlines | Ontario, California | Crashed during training flight |
| Jul 25, 1971 | 707-321C | N461PA | Pan American | Manila, Philippines | Crashed on approach |
| Dec 15, 1971 | 707-340C | AP-AVZ | PIA | Near Ürümqi, China | Crashed |
| Mar 8, 1972 | 707-331 | N761TW | TWA | Las Vegas, Nevada | Damaged beyond repair |
| Sep 14, 1972 | 707-331C | N15712 | TWA | San Francisco IAP, California | Crashed into San Francisco Bay following aborted take-off |
| Dec 5, 1972 | 707-366C | SU-AOW | EgyptAir | South of Cairo, Egypt | Crashed |
| Jan 2, 1973 | 707-321C | CF-PWZ | Pacific Western Airlines | Near Edmonton, Canada | Crashed |
| Jan 22, 1973 | 707-3D3C | JY-ADO | Alia-Royal Jordanian | Kano AP, Nigeria | Crashed on landing |
| Jun 9, 1973 | 707-327C | PP-VLJ | VARIG | Galeão IAP, Rio de Janeiro, Brazil | Crashed on landing |
| Jul 11, 1973 | 707-345C | PP-VJZ | VARIG | Paris-Orly AP, France | Crashed on approach |
| Jul 22, 1973 | 707-321B | N417PA | Pan American | Off Papeete, Tahiti, French Polynesia | Crashed into sea on take-off |
| Nov 3, 1973 | 707-321C | N458PA | Pan American | Boston, Massachusetts | Crashed on landing |
| Dec 17, 1973 | 707-321B | N407PA | Pan American | Rome-Fiumicino IAP, Italy | Terrorist attack |
| Dec 20, 1973 | 707-330B | D-ABOT | Lufthansa | Near New Delhi, India | Crashed on approach to Palam AP, Delhi |
| Jan 16, 1974 | 707-131B | N757TW | TWA | Los Angeles IAP, California | Damaged beyond repair in landing accident |
| Jan 30, 1974 | 707-321B | N454PA | Pan American | Pago Pago, American Samoa | Crashed |
| Apr 22, 1974 | 707-321C | N446PA | Pan American | Near Singajara, Bali, Indonesia | Crashed |
| Sep 8, 1974 | 707-331B | N8734 | TWA | Ionian Sea | Crashed |
| Sep 13, 1974 | 720-025 | OY-DSR | Conair of Scandinavia | Kastrup AP, Copenhagen, Denmark | Damaged beyond repair in landing accident |
| Aug 3, 1975 | 707-321C | JY-AEE | Alia-Royal Jordanian | Near Agadir, Morocco | Crashed |

G-APFE, the fifth 707-436 for BOAC, crashed on Mount Fuji, Japan, on March 5, 1966. *Boeing, courtesy of Peter M. Bowers*

| Date | Model | Registration | Operator | Location | Circumstance |
|------|-------|--------------|----------|----------|--------------|
| Dec 22, 1975 | 707-331B | N18701 | TWA | Malpensa AP, Milan, Italy | Crashed |
| Jan 1, 1976 | 720-023B | OD-AFT | MEA | Al Qaysumah, Saudi Arabia | Crashed |
| Apr 22, 1976 | 720-022 | N37777 | U.S. Global of Florida | Near Barranquilla, Colombia | Crashed |
| Jun 27, 1976 | 720-047B | OD-AGE | MEA | Beirut IAP, Lebanon | Destroyed in shelling of airport |
| Aug 2, 1976 | 707-373C | HL7412 | Korean Air | Near Teheran, Iran | Crashed into mountain |
| Aug 16, 1976 | 720-047B | HK-723 | AVIANCA | Benito Juárez IAP, Mexico City, Mexico | Damaged beyond repair in landing accident |
| Sep 7, 1976 | 707-328 | F-BHSH | Air France | Ajaccio-Campo dell'Oro AP, Corsica, France | Terrorist bomb |
| Oct 13, 1976 | 707-131 | N730JP | Lloyd Aero Boliviano | Santa Cruz, Bolivia | Crashed on take-off |
| Dec 25, 1976 | 707-366C | SU-AXA | EgyptAir | Bangkok, Thailand | Crashed on approach to Don Muang AP |
| Mar 17, 1977 | 707-436 | G-APFK | British Airtours | Prestwick, Scotland, UK | Crashed during crew training |
| May 14, 1977 | 707-321C | G-BEBP | IAS Cargo Airlines | Near Lusaka, Zambia | Crashed on approach |
| Aug 9, 1977 | 707-430 | 9Q-CRT | Pearl Air | San'a IAP, Yemen | Damaged beyond repair |
| Nov 19, 1977 | 707-360C | ET-ACD | Ethiopian Airlines | Rome-Fiumicino AP, Italy | Crashed on take-off |
| Feb 15, 1978 | 707-329 | OO-SJE | SABENA | Tenerife AP, Canary Islands, Spain | Crashed on landing |
| Apr 2, 1978 | 707-321B | HL7429 | Korean Air | Near Murmansk, USSR | Shot down by Soviet fighters |
| Aug 3, 1978 | 707-351B | CC-CCX | LAN-Chile | Buenos Aires, Argentina | Crashed on landing at Ezeiza AP |
| Jan 30, 1979 | 707-323C | PP-VLU | VARIG | Off Tokyo, Japan | Crashed into sea on take-off |
| Apr 1, 1979 | 707-321C | 5X-UAL | Uganda Airlines | Entebbe AP, Uganda | Destroyed on the ground during war between Uganda and Tanzania |
| Jul 23, 1979 | 707-327C | OD-AFX | TMA | Beirut, Lebanon | Crashed during training flight |
| Jul 26, 1979 | 707-330C | D-ABUY | Lufthansa | Petropolis, Brazil | Crashed |
| Aug 19, 1979 | 707-123B | 5B-DAM | Cyprus Airways | Bahrain IAP, Bahrain | Damaged beyond repair after nosewheel collapsed |
| Sep 11, 1979 | 707-324C | B-1834 | China Airlines | Near Taipei, Taiwan | Crashed during training flight |
| Nov 26, 1979 | 707-340C | AP-AWZ | PIA | Saudi Arabia | Crashed 125 kilometers from Jeddah |
| Nov [?], 1979 | 707-373C | HZ-ACE | Saudia | Jeddah, Saudi Arabia | Damaged beyond repair in heavy landing |
| Jan 27, 1980 | 720-059B | HK-725 | AVIANCA | Mariscal Sucre IAP, Quito, Ecuador | Damaged beyond repair in landing accident |
| Feb 27, 1980 | 707-309C | B-1826 | China Airlines | Manila IAP, Philippines | Ground fire |
| Apr 4, 1980 | 707-373C | S2-ABQ | Bangladesh Biman | Singapore | Damaged beyond repair |

VT-DJI, a 707-437 of Air India was destroyed on January 23, 1971 when it overran the runway at the Bombay Airport. *Foto-Flash*

| Date | Model | Registration | Operator | Location | Circumstance |
|------|-------|-------------|----------|----------|--------------|
| May 11, 1980 | 707-329C | OO-SJH | Zaire International Air Cargo | Douala AP, Cameroon | Landing accident |
| Nov 30, 1980 | 707-131B | N797TW | TWA | San Francisco IAP, California | Damaged beyond repair in landing accident |
| Dec 20, 1980 | 707-321 | HK-2410 | Aerotal Colombia | El Dorado IAP, Bogotá, Colombia | Destroyed by fire following heavy landing |
| Jan 8, 1981 | 720-047B | AP-AXK | PIA | Quetta, Pakistan | Damaged beyond repair |
| Jun 11, 1981 | 707-341C | PP-VJT | VARIG | Eduardo Gomes IAP, Manaus, Brazil | Damaged beyond repair |
| July 7, 1981 | 707-327C | OD-AGW | TMA | Beirut IAP, Lebanon | Destroyed in shelling of airport |
| Aug 31, 1981 | 720-023B | OD-AFR | MEA | Beirut IAP, Lebanon | Sabotage on the ground |
| Oct 23, 1981 | 707-331C | OD-AGT | TMA | Narita IAP, Tokyo, Japan | Damaged beyond repair |
| Dec 12, 1981 | 707-124 | HI-384HA | Hispaniola Airways | Miami IAP, Florida | Damaged beyond repair in landing accident |
| Jan 26, 1982 | 707-348C | 7O-ACJ | Alyemda | Damascus AP, Syria | Damaged beyond repair in landing accident |
| Jun 12, 1982 | 707-3B4C | OD-AFB | MEA | Beirut IAP, Lebanon | Damaged beyond repair in Israeli shelling of airport |
| Jun 12, 1982 | 720-023B | OD-AFP | MEA | Beirut IAP, Lebanon | Destroyed in Israeli shelling of airport |
| Jun 16, 1982 | 720-023B | OD-AFU | MEA | Beirut IAP, Lebanon | Destroyed in Israeli shelling of airport |
| Jun 16, 1982 | 720-023B | OD-AFW | MEA | Beirut IAP, Lebanon | Destroyed in Israeli shelling of airport |
| Jun 16, 1982 | 707-323C | OD-AGN | MEA | Beirut IAP, Lebanon | Destroyed in Israeli shelling of airport |

TWA lost 11 Boeing 707s: one -131, two -131Bs, two -331s, three -331Bs, and three -331Cs. Photographed at Boeing Field, this 707-331B displays its spoilers in the up position. *Boeing, courtesy of Peter M. Bowers*

This ex-TWA 707-331C was damaged beyond repair at the Narita International Airport in Japan on October 23, 1981 while leased from Guinness Peat Aviation by Trans Mediterranean Airways. *Jelle Sjoerdsma*

This spectacular crash was staged by NASA at Edwards AFB, California, on December 1, 1984. This 720-027 was radio-controlled into obstacles at the end of the runway during NASA's evaluation of a new fuel additive designed to lessen the hazards associated with burning fuel during an aircraft accident. Clearly, the additive did not prove effective. *NASA*

| Date | Model | Registration | Operator | Location | Circumstance |
|---|---|---|---|---|---|
| Jun 16, 1982 | 720-047B | OD-AGR | MEA | Beirut IAP, Lebanon | Destroyed in Israeli shelling of airport |
| Aug 1, 1982 | 720-047B | OD-AGG | MEA | Beirut IAP, Lebanon | Damaged beyond repair by Israeli bombs |
| Sep 10, 1982 | 707-348C | ST-AIM | Sudan Airways | Near Khartoum, Sudan | Crashed into River Nile |
| Oct 17, 1982 | 707-366C | SU-APD | EgyptAir | Cointrin AP, Geneva, Switzerland | Crashed |
| Dec 4, 1982 | 707-323B | N8434 | Global International Airways | Brasilia IAP, Brazil | Damaged beyond repair in wheels-up landing |
| Mar 14, 1983 | 707-338C | 5A-DJO | United African Airlines | Sheba, Libya | Engine explosion on take-off |
| Jun [?] 1983 | 720-023B | OD-AFO | MEA | Beirut IAP, Lebanon | Damaged beyond repair |
| Sep 25, 1983 | 707-336C | 5N-ARO | RN Cargo of Nigeria | Accra AP, Ghana | Ground fire |
| Oct 13, 1983 | 707-436 | N4465D | Coastal Airways | Perpignan AP, France | Ground fire |
| Dec 14, 1983 | 707-373C | HK-2401X | TAMPA Colombia | Olaya Herrera AP, Medellín, Colombia | Crashed on take-off after engine failure |
| Dec 1, 1984 | 720-027 | N833NA | NASA | Edwards AFB, California | Intentionally crashed while radio-controlled in Impact Demonstration test |
| Jun 13, 1985 | 707-336B | TY-BBR | Benin Government | Sheba AP, Libya | Destroyed by fire following aborted take-off |
| Aug 21, 1985 | 720-023B | OD-AFL | MEA | Beirut IAP, Lebanon | Destroyed in shelling of airport |
| Aug 21, 1985 | 720-047B | OD-AGQ | MEA | Beirut IAP, Lebanon | Destroyed in shelling of airport |
| Jan 3, 1987 | 707-379C | PP-VJK | VARIG | Pointe Alepe, Côte d'Ivoire | Crashed |
| Jan 8, 1987 | 707-323C | OD-AHB | MEA | Beirut IAP, Lebanon | Destroyed in shelling of airport |
| Apr 11, 1987 | 707-330C | PT-TCO | Transbrasil | Eduardo Gomes IAP, Manaus, Brazil | Damaged beyond repair |
| Apr 13, 1987 | 707-351C | N144SP | Burlington Air Express | Kansas City, Missouri | Crashed on approach to Kansas City IAP |
| Nov 29, 1987 | 707-3B5C | HL7406 | Korean Air | Andaman Sea off Thailand | Crashed on approach to Don Muang AP |
| Feb 8, 1988 | 707-349C | D2-TOI | TAAG Angola Airlines | Luanda AP, Angola | Damaged beyond repair in landing accident |
| Jul 21, 1988 | 707-328C | D2-TOV | TAAG Angolan Air Charter | Near Lagos, Nigeria | Crashed |
| Oct 10, 1988 | 707-347C | D2-TOM | TAAG Angola Airlines | Luanda AP, Angola | Ground fire |
| Oct 17, 1988 | 707-338C | 5X-UBC | Uganda Airlines | Rome-Fiumicino AP, Italy | Crashed on approach |
| Dec 14, 1988 | 707-351C | 5N-AYJ | Gas Air Nigeria | Kom-Omran, Egypt | Crashed |
| Feb 8, 1989 | 707-331B | N7231T | Independent Air | Santa Maria, Azores, Portugal | Crashed |
| Mar 21, 1989 | 707-349C | PT-TCS | Transbrasil | São Paulo, Brazil | Crashed on approach to Guarulhos IAP |
| May 17, 1989 | 707-330B | 60-SBT | Somali Airlines | Jomo Kenyatta IAP, Nairobi, Kenya | Damaged beyond repair in take-off accident |
| Jul 11, 1989 | 707-351B | 5Y-BBK | Kenya Airways | Addis Ababa AP, Ethiopia | Damaged beyond repair in landing accident |
| Jan 25, 1990 | 707-321B | HK-2016 | AVIANCA | Long Island, New York | Crashed after running out of fuel |
| Mar 1, 1990 | 707-329C | OO-SJJ | Katela Aero Transport | Goma AP, Zaire | Damaged beyond repair in landing accident |

S/N B-2402, B-2402, was destroyed on October 2, 1990 when a 737-247 (S/N 23189, B-2510) crashed into it at the Guangzhou Airport in the People's Republic of China. *Boeing*

HK-3355C, an ex-Continental Airlines 707-324C, was damaged beyond repair at the Guarulhos Airport in São Paulo, Brazil, on October 9, 1994. *Kevin Cook*

| Date | Model | Registration | Operator | Location | Circumstance |
|------|-------|--------------|----------|----------|--------------|
| Jun 23, 1990 | 707-321B | CC-CEI | LAN Chile | Pudahuel IAP, Santiago, Chile | Ground towing accident |
| Jul 14, 1990 | 707-349C | ST-ALK | Trans Arabian Air Transport | Khartoum AP, Sudan | Damaged beyond repair in landing accident |
| Jul 25, 1990 | 707-379C | ET-ACQ | Ethiopian Airlines | Addis Ababa AP, Ethiopia | Aborted take-off |
| Sep 20, 1990 | 707-321B | N320MJ | Omega Air | Marana AP, Arizona | Crashed on take-off |
| Oct 2, 1990 | 707-3J6B | B-2402 | China Southwest Airlines | Guangzhou AP, China | Hit on the ground by 737 |
| Dec 4, 1990 | 707-321C | ST-SAC | Sudania Air Cargo | Nairobi, Kenya | Crashed on approach to Jomo Kenyatta IAP |
| Jan 10, 1991 | 707-3K1C | YR-ABD | Tarom | Otopeni AP, Bucharest, Romania | Damaged beyond repair in landing accident |
| Mar 25, 1991 | 707-385C | ET-AJZ | Ethiopian Airlines | Asmara, Ethiopia | Destroyed by shelling during civil war |
| Aug 31, 1991 | 707-323C | CP-1365 | Lloyd Aero Boliviano | Dotham, Alabama | Hangar fire |
| Oct 29, 1991 | 707-368C | A20-103 | RAAF | Vicinity of East Sale, Australia | Crashed during training flight |
| Dec 1, 1991 | 707-351C | 5Y-BFB | ZAS Airline | unknown | Crashed |
| Dec 9, 1991 | 707-351C | 5A-DJU | Libyan Arab Airlines | Tripoli AP, Libya | Landing accident |
| Mar 24, 1992 | 707-321C | SY-ALX | Golden Star Air Cargo | Mount Hymittus, Greece | Crashed into mountain |
| Mar 31, 1992 | 707-321C | 5N-MAS | Kabo Air | Istres-Le Tubé AB, France | Damaged beyond repair after losing two engines in flight |
| Apr 29, 1992 | 707-351C | 9G-RBO | Gas Air Nigeria | Ilorin, Nigeria | Damaged beyond repair after gear up landing |
| Nov 25, 1992 | 707-321C | 5X-DAR | Dairo Air Service | Kano, Nigeria | Crashed on approach |
| Nov 26, 1992 | 707-365C | PT-TCP | Aerobrasil | Eduardo Gomes IAP, Manaus, Brazil | Damaged beyond repair in take-off accident |
| Jan 15, 1993 | 707-321C | YR-ABM | Air Afrique | Abidjan, Côte d'Ivoire | Damaged beyond repair in landing accident |
| Jan 31, 1993 | 707-387B | LV-ISA | Lineas Aereas del Estado | Recife, Brazil | Damaged beyond repair in landing accident |
| Jul 26, 1993 | 707-327C | OD-AFY | TMA | Schiphol IAP, Amsterdam, Netherlands | Damaged beyond repair in landing accident |
| Oct 9, 1994 | 707-324C | HK-3355X | TAMPA Colombia | Guarulhos IAP, São Paulo, Brazil | Damaged beyond repair in landing accident |
| Dec 20, 1994 | 707-3F9C | 5N-ABK | Nigeria Airways | Lagos, Nigeria | Crashed shortly after take-off from Murtala Mohammed AP |
| Aug 17, 1995 | 707-321C | YR-ABN | Air Afrique | N'Djamena, Chad | Crashed on landing |
| Sep 22, 1995 | E-3B | 77-0354 | USAF | Elmendorf AFB, Alaska | Crashed after ingesting birds on take-off |
| Nov 30, 1995 | 707-323C | 4K-401 | Azerbaijan Airlines | Near Baku, Azerbaijan | Crashed on approach |
| Jun 30, 1996 | 707-369C | 5X-JON | Air Afrique | Bamako, Mali | Crashed on landing |
| Jul 17, 1996 | E-3A | LX-N90457 | NATO | FOB Aktion, Greece | Damaged beyond repair in take-off accident |
| Aug 21, 1996 | 707-366C | SU-AVX | EgyptAir | Yesilköy AP, Istanbul, Turkey | Damaged beyond repair in landing accident |
| Oct 23, 1996 | 707-323C | N751MA | Million Air | Manta, Ecuador | Crashed on take-off |
| Oct 23, 1996 | 707-372C | TC-92 | Fuerza Aerea Argentina | Ezeiza AP, Buenos Aires, Argentina | Damaged beyond repair in landing accident |
| Jan 16, 1997 | 707-331C | P4-OOOO | First International Airlines | Ndjili AP, Kinshasa, Zaire | Damaged beyond repair in landing accident |

# APPENDIX 2: 707 AND 720 POWER PLANTS

## Pratt & Whitney JT3C Models for the 707-120 & 720-020 Series and J57 for Military C-135 Variants

| Model | TO Rating (lb thrust) | Max Continuous Rating (lb thrust) | Weight (lb) | Diameter (in) | Length (in) | Application |
|---|---|---|---|---|---|---|
| JT3L | 9,500 (Dry) 11,100 (Wet) | 8,250 | 4,160 | 41.00 | 159.30 | Proposed for the 367-80. Not built. |
| JT3P | 9,500 (Dry) 11,000 (Wet) | 8,250 | 4,220 | 40.50 | 157.70 | Initial installation in the 367-80. |
| JT3C-4 | 11,200 (Dry) 12,500 (Wet) | 9,000 | 4,234 | 38.88 | 138.64 | Later installation in the 367-80. |
| JT3C-5 | 11,200 (Dry) 13,750 (Wet) | 9,000 | 4,350 | 40.50 | N/A | Proposed for the 707-120. |
| JT3C-6 | 11,200 (Dry) 13,000 (Wet) | 10,000 | 4,234 | 38.88 | 138.64 | 707-120 |
| JT3C-6 Advanced | 11,200 (Dry) 13,500 (Wet) | 10,000 | 4,234 | 38.88 | 138.64 | 707-120 |

The inboard JT3Ps of the 367-80 were replaced by a JT4A-3 in the number 2 position and a JT3C-4 in the number 3 position in December 1957. The JT3C-4 was replaced by a JT3C-6 in April 1958. As part of the Boeing 727 development program, a JT3C-4 was added on the left side of the rear fuselage in April 1961 and was replaced by a JT8D1 in January 1962. *Boeing*

| Model | TO Rating (lb thrust) | Max Continuous Rating (lb thrust) | Weight (lb) | Diameter (in) | Length (in) | Application |
|---|---|---|---|---|---|---|
| JT3C-7 | 12,000 (Dry) | 10,000 | 3,495 | 38.80 | 136.78 | 720-020 |
| JT3C-10 | 10,200 (Dry) 13,000 (Wet) | 9,500 | 3,695 | 38.88 | 167.20 | Proposed for the 707-120. Not built. |
| JT3C-12 | 11,500 (Dry) 13,000 (Wet) | 11,500 | 3,550 | 38.88 | 136.78 | 720-020 |
| J57-P-29WB | 10,500 (Dry) 12,100 (Wet) | | 4,150 | 40.50 | 157.52 | First three KC-135As. |
| J57-P-43W & J57-F-43W | 11,200 (Dry) 13,750 (Wet) | | 3,870 | 38.88 | 138.58 | KC-135A & derivatives |
| J57-P-59W & J57-F-59W | 11,200 (Dry) 13,750 (Wet) | | 4,320 | 38.88 | 167.33 | KC-135A/Q & derivatives C-135A & derivatives |

SOURCE: Type Certificate Data Sheet Nos. 4A21 and 4A28, Federal Aviation Administration.
*Engine Listings Manual,* Pratt & Whitney Aircraft Group, December 1976 revision.

With water injection, civil JT3Cs and military J57s were particularly noisy engines. Much of the development work undertaken with the 367-80 was devoted to testing a variety of engine noise suppressors. *Boeing, courtesy of Peter M. Bowers*

This 707-344 of South African Airways/Suid-Afrikaanse Lugdiens carries a spare JT4A-11 in a nacelle under the left wing root. *Boeing, courtesy of Peter M. Bowers*

## Pratt & Whitney JT3D Models for the 707-120B, 707-320B, 707-320C & 720-020B Series and TF33 for Military C-135 & 707 Variants

| Model | TO Rating (lb thrust) | Max Continuous Rating (lb thrust) | Weight (lb) | Diameter (in) | Length (in) | Application |
|---|---|---|---|---|---|---|
| JT3D-1 | 17,000 (Dry) | 14,500 | 4,130 | 53.10 | 136.3 | 707-120B, 707-320C & 720-020B |
| JT3D-1-MC6 | 17,000 (Dry) | 14,500 | 4,540 | 53.10 | 145.5 | JT3C-6 turbojets rebuilt as turbofans for the 707-120B & 707-320C |
| JT3D-1-MC7 | 17,000 (Dry) | 14,500 | 4,165 | 53.00 | 167.7 | JT3C-7 turbojets rebuilt as turbofans for the 707-120B, 707-320C & 720-020B |
| JT3D-3 | 18,000 (Dry) | 16,400 | 4,170 | 53.10 | 136.3 | 707-120B, 707-320B & 707-320C |
| JT3D-3B | 18,000 (Dry) | 16,400 | 4,300 | 53.10 | 136.3 | 707-120B, 707-320B & 707-320C |
| JT3D-7 | 19,000 (Dry) | 17,200 | 4,300 | 53.10 | 136.3 | 707-320B & 707-320C |
| TF33-P-5 | 18,000 (Dry) | 16,400 | 4,275 | 53.14 | 137.423 | C-135B, WC-135B, RC-135E & derivatives |
| TF33-P-9 | 18,000 (Dry) | 16,400 | 4,170 | 53.14 | 137.423 | KC-135B |
| TF33-PW-100A | 21,000 (Dry) | 18,000 | 4,790 | 54.06 | 142 | USAF E-3 |
| TF33-PW-102 | 18,000 (Dry) | 16,400 | 4,300 | 53.10 | 136.3 | Re-engined C/KC-135 variants and C-18 variants |

SOURCE:    Type Certificate Data Sheet Nos. 4A21, 4A26, and 4A28, Federal Aviation Administration.
*Engine Listings Manual,* Pratt & Whitney Aircraft Group, December 1976 revision.

The number 3 nacelle of a French E-3F housing a CFM56-2B1. *René J. Francillon*

## Pratt & Whitney JT4A Models for the 707-220 & 707-320 Series

| Model | TO Rating (lb thrust) | Max Continuous Rating (lb thrust) | Weight (lb) | Diameter (in) | Length (in) | Application |
|---|---|---|---|---|---|---|
| JT4A-3 | 15,800 (Dry) | 12,500 | 5,020 | 43.0 | 144.1 | 707-220 & 707-320 |
| JT4-5 | 15,800 (Dry) | 12,500 | 4,815 | 43.0 | 144.1 | 707-320 |
| JT4A-9 | 16,800 (Dry) | 13,500 | 5,050 | 43.0 | 144.1 | 707-320 |
| JT4A-11 | 17,500 (Dry) | 14,900 | 5,100 | 43.0 | 144.1 | 707-320 |
| JT4A-12 | 17,500 (Dry) | 14,900 | 4,895 | 43.0 | 144.1 | 707-320 |

SOURCE: Type Certificate Data Sheet No. 4A26, Federal Aviation Administration.
*Engine Listings Manual,* Pratt & Whitney Aircraft Group, December 1976 revision.

## Rolls-Royce Conway for the 707-420 Series

| Model | TO Rating (lb thrust) | Max Continuous Rating (lb thrust) | Weight (lb) | Diameter (in) | Length (in) | Application |
|---|---|---|---|---|---|---|
| Conway Mark 508 (R.Co.12) | 17,500 (Dry) | 14,625 | 4,544 | 42.0 | 136.0 | 707-420 |

SOURCE: Type Certificate Data Sheet No. 4A26, Federal Aviation Administration.
*Jane's All the World's Aircraft,* 1968–1969.

## CFM International CFM56 for the 707-700 and Re-Engined C-135 & Military 707 Derivatives

| Model | TO Rating (lb thrust) | Weight (lb) | Diameter (in) | Length (in) | Application |
|---|---|---|---|---|---|
| CFM56-1 | 22,000 (Dry) | 4,420 | 72 | 95.7 | 707-700 |
| CFM56-2A | 24,000 (Dry) | 4,820 | 68.3 | 95.7 | Export E-3 & E-8B |
| CFM65-2B1/ F108-CF-100 | 22,000 (Dry) | 4,674 | 68.3 | 95.7 | Re-engined C/KC-135 variants |

SOURCE: *Jane's All the World's Aircraft,* 1979–1980 & 1991–1992.

# APPENDIX 3: BOEING 707 AND 720 PRODUCTION SUMMARY

| | | Civil | Military/ Government | Total |
|---|---|---|---|---|
| **367-80** | | | | |
| -80 | Boeing | 1 | | |
| | Sub-total | 1 | 0 | 1 |
| **707-120** | | | | |
| -121 | Pan American | 6 | | |
| -123 | American | 25 | | |
| -124 | Continental | 5 | | |
| -131 | TWA | 15 | | |
| -138 | Qantas | 7 | | |
| -139 | Cubana/Western | 2 | | |
| -153 | USAF (VC-137A) | | 3 | |
| | Sub-total | 60 | 3 | 63 |
| **707-120B** | | | | |
| -123B | American | 31 | | |
| -131B | TWA | 41 | | |
| -138B | Qantas | 6 | | |
| | Sub-total | 78 | 0 | 78 |
| **707-220** | | | | |
| -227 | Braniff | 5 | | |
| | Sub-total | 5 | 0 | 5 |
| **707-320** | | | | |
| -321 | Pan American | 20 | | |
| -328 | Air France | 21 | | |
| -329 | SABENA | 7 | | |
| -331 | TWA | 12 | | |

Cubana de Aviación ordered two 707-139s in June 1957. However, before these aircraft could be delivered, the new Fidel Castro regime fell afoul with the United States. The aircraft were delivered as N74613 (illustrated) and N74614 to Western Airlines. *Boeing*

| | | Civil | Military/Government | Total |
|---|---|---|---|---|
| -331 | Pan American | 6 | | |
| -344 | SAA | 3 | | |
| | Sub-total | 69 | 0 | 69 |
| **707-320B** | | | | |
| -312B | Malaysian-Singapore | 3 | | |
| -321B | Pan American | 60 | | |
| -323B | American | 10 | | |
| -328B | Air France | 8 | | |
| -330B | Lufthansa | 12 | | |
| -331B | TWA | 38 | | |
| -336B | BOAC | 2 | | |
| -337B | Air India | 3 | | |
| -344B | SAA | 2 | | |
| -351B | Northwest | 10 | | |
| -353B | USAF (VC-137C) | | 2 | |
| -358B | El Al | 3 | | |
| -359B | AVIANCA | 2 | | |
| -382B | TAP | 7 | | |
| -384B | Olympic | 2 | | |
| -387B | Aerolineas Argentinas | 4 | | |
| -3F3B | Argentine Government | | 1 | |
| -3J6B | CAAC | 4 | | |

| | | Civil | Military/<br>Government | Total |
|---|---|---|---|---|
| -3L6B | Malaysian Government | | 1 | |
| -320B | USAF (EC-137D) | | 2 | |
| -320B | USAF (E-3A) | | 22 | |
| -320B | USAF (E-3B) | | 10 | |
| -320B | Royal Saudi Air Force (E-3A) | | 5 | |
| -320B | Royal Saudi Air Force (KE-3A) | | 8 | |
| -320B | Royal Air Force (E-3D) | | 7 | |
| -320B | Armée de l'air (E-3F) | | 4 | |
| -320B | NATO (E-3A) | | 18 | |
| | Sub-total | 170 | 80 | 250 |
| **707-320C** | | | | |
| -307C | Luftwaffe | | 4 | |
| -309C | China Airlines | 2 | | |
| -311C | Wardair | 1 | | |
| -320C | Boeing | 1 | | |
| -321C | Pan American | 34 | | |
| -321C | Continental | 2 | | |
| -323C | American | 36 | | |
| -324C | Continental | 11 | | |
| -327C | Braniff | 9 | | |
| -328C | Air France | 8 | | |
| -329C | SABENA | 7 | | |
| -330C | Lufthansa | 6 | | |
| -331C | TWA | 15 | | |

Delivered to American Airlines on September 9, 1969, this 707-323B was acquired by Ports of Call in September 1983. It was on lease to Skyworld Airlines when photographed at Norton AFB, California, in January 1989. *Marty Isham*

Southern Air Transport acquired S/N 20084, a 707-369C, from Kuwait Airways in November 1985. *Geoff LeBaron, courtesy of Marty Isham*

| | | Civil | Military/<br>Government | Total |
|---|---|---|---|---|
| -336C | BOAC | 7 | | |
| -337C | Air India | 2 | | |
| -338C | Qantas | 21 | | |
| -340C | PIA | 7 | | |
| -341C | VARIG | 3 | | |
| -344C | SAA | 5 | | |
| -345C | VARIG | 3 | | |
| -347C | Western | 5 | | |
| -347C | Canadian Forces | | 5 | |
| -348C | Aer Lingus | 4 | | |
| -349C | Flying Tiger | 4 | | |
| -351C | Northwest | 26 | | |
| -355C | Air France | 1 | | |
| -355C | Executive Jet | 2 | | |
| -358C | El Al | 2 | | |
| -360C | Ethiopian | 1 | | |
| -365C | Caledonian Airways | 1 | | |
| -365C | British Eagle | 1 | | |
| -366C | EgyptAir | 9 | | |
| -366C | Egyptian Government | | 1 | |
| -368C | Saudi Arabian | 7 | | |
| -368C | Kingdom of Saudi Arabia | | 1 | |
| -369C | Kuwait | 5 | | |
| -370C | Iraqi Airways | 3 | | |
| -372C | Airlift International | 2 | | |
| -373C | World Airways | 9 | | |
| -373C | TWA | 2 | | |
| -379C | BOAC | 1 | | |

| | | Civil | Military/ Government | Total |
|---|---|---|---|---|
| -379C | Ethiopian | 1 | | |
| -379C | VARIG | 1 | | |
| -384C | Olympic | 4 | | |
| -385C | Boeing | 1 | | |
| -385C | American | 1 | | |
| -386C | Iranair | 4 | | |
| -387C | Aerolineas Argentinas | 2 | | |
| -396C | Wardair | 1 | | |
| -399C | British Caledonian | 2 | | |
| -3B4C | MEA | 4 | | |
| -3B5C | Korean Air | 1 | | |
| -3D3C | Alia-Royal Jordanian | 2 | | |
| -3F5C | Portuguese Air Force | | 2 | |
| -3F9C | Nigeria | 3 | | |
| -3H7C | Camair | 1 | | |
| -3J6C | CAAC | 6 | | |
| -3J8C | Sudan Air | 2 | | |
| -3J9C | Imperial Iranian Air Force | | 14 | |
| -3K1C | Tarom | 4 | | |
| -3L5C | Libyan Arab | 1 | | |
| -3L6C | Aviation Services & Support | 1 | | |
| -3M1C | Pertamina/Indonesian Government | | | 1 |
| -3P1C | Qatar Emiri | | 1 | |
| -3W6C | Moroccan Gov't (rebuilt 707-700) | | | (1) |
| -320C | USN (E-6A) | | 16 | |
| -320C | USAF (E-8B) | | 1 | |
| | Sub-total | 307 | 46 | 353 |

**707-420**

| | | Civil | Military/ Government | Total |
|---|---|---|---|---|
| -430 | Lufthansa | 5 | | |
| -436 | BOAC | 16 | | |
| -436 | BOAC-Cunard | 2 | | |
| -437 | Air India | 6 | | |
| -441 | VARIG | 3 | | |
| -458 | El Al | 3 | | |
| -465 | Cunard Eagle | 1 | | |
| -465 | BOAC | 1 | | |
| | Sub-total | 37 | 0 | 37 |

**707-700**

| | | Civil | Military/ Government | Total |
|---|---|---|---|---|
| -700 | Boeing | 1 | | |

*(Refurbished as 707-3W6C for the Moroccan government)*

| | | Civil | Military/ Government | Total |
|---|---|---|---|---|
| | Sub-total | 1 | 0 | 1 |
| | **Total 707 series** | **728** | **129** | **857** |

720

Braniff International Airways ordered three 720-027s in March 1960, one in April 1961, and one in June 1962. The second of these aircraft, S/N 18065, N7077, lands at Boeing Field. *Boeing*

| | | Civil | Military/ Government | Total |
|---|---|---|---|---|
| -022 | United | 29 | | |
| -023 | American | 10 | | |
| -025 | Eastern | 15 | | |
| -027 | Braniff | 5 | | |
| -027 | FAA | | 1 | |
| -048 | Aer Lingus | 3 | | |
| -062 | Pacific Northern | 2 | | |
| | Sub-total | 64 | 1 | 65 |
| **720B** | | | | |
| -023B | American | 12 | | |
| -023B | Pan American | 3 | | |
| -024B | Continental | 8 | | |
| -030B | Lufthansa | 8 | | |
| -040B | PIA | 4 | | |
| -047B | Western | 27 | | |
| -051B | Northwest | 17 | | |
| -058B | El Al | 2 | | |
| -059B | AVIANCA | 3 | | |
| -060B | Ethiopian | 3 | | |
| -068B | Saudi Arabian | 2 | | |
| | Sub-total | 89 | 0 | 89 |
| | **Total 720 series** | **153** | **1** | **154** |
| **Grand total 367-80/707/720** | | **881** | **130** | **1,011** |

# INDEX

# MODEL INDEX